Margaret Drabble

Twayne's English Authors Series

Kinley E. Roby, Editor

Northeastern University

TEAS 417

MARGARET DRABBLE.
Photograph by Mark Gerson
and reprinted by his permission.

Margaret Drabble

By Lynn Veach Sadler

Methodist College

Twayne Publishers • *Boston*

Margaret Drabble

Lynn Veach Sadler

Copyright © 1986 by G. K. Hall & Co.
All Rights Reserved
Published by Twayne Publishers
A Division of G. K. Hall & Co.
70 Lincoln Street
Boston, Massachusetts 02111

Copyediting supervised by Lewis DeSimone
Book production by Lyda E. Kuth
Book design by Barbara Anderson

Typeset in 11 pt. Garamond
by Modern Graphics Inc., Weymouth, Massachusetts

Printed on permanent/durable acid-free paper
and bound in the United States of America.

Library of Congress Cataloging in Publication Data

Sadler, Lynn Veach.
  Margaret Drabble.

  (Twayne's English authors series; TEAS 417)
  Bibliography: p. 141
  Includes index.
  1. Drabble, Margaret, 1939–
  —Criticism and interpretation.
  I. Title.   II. Series.
PR6054.R25Z89   1986   823′.914   95–17732
ISBN 0–8057–6907–2
ISBN 0–8057–6926–9 (pbk.)

Contents

About the Author

Mary Lynn Veach Sadler was graduated from Duke University *magna cum laude*. She received an M.A. and a Ph.D. from the University of Illinois. She has held a postdoctoral research grant from the Clark Library and UCLA for work on Milton, has a certificate in administration from Bryn Mawr College and Higher Education Resource Services, and has studied at Oxford.

Dr. Sadler has taught at Agnes Scott College, Drake University, North Carolina Agricultural and Technical State University, and Bennett College, where she was chair of the Department of Communications and director of the Division of Humanities. She is now the vice president for academic affairs at Methodist College in Fayetteville, North Carolina. She received an award for "Extraordinary Undergraduate Teaching" from Drake University.

Her publications include books on Bunyan, Carew, and Milton. In the summer of 1984 she directed a National Endowment for the Humanities summer seminar for college professors on "The Novel of Slave Unrest." Additional interests are creative writing and educational computing.

Preface

Margaret Drabble exasperates and delights me. I had difficulty not slamming *The Waterfall* on the floor. I do not want women to be like turn-her-face-to-the-wall Jane or stiff-upper-lip Rosamund or Bible-in-the-mind-toting Rose. I wish Drabble had not given so many interviews; I seldom agree with her views of her characters. She apologizes for the earliest novels; I find *A Summer Bird-Cage* one of the most refreshing books in years. I understand why Clara Maugham is as she is; I wish Drabble would stop criticizing her. I tire a bit of the "Drabble woman," *au fait,* "the real thing," "cultivating one's garden," aureate imagery, inconclusiveness, cuteness of style, emphasis on the past, succoring the unlovely, solipsism, privilege, grace, fate, chance, and luck.

I am embarrassed that Drabble still gets proclaimed the queen of motherhood and children, but she ought not to be appropriated by the feminists either. She refutes their claims to her—while publicly wanting England to establish a Woman's Union and denying androgyny but insisting that one of her favorites, Angus Wilson, is as nearly androgynous as a writer can be. I like most of her men.

I also like Frances wearing Karel's teeth in her brassiere and all the other such little gems of humor and wildness in Drabble's novels. I like her liking John Milton, John Bunyan, and William Wordsworth and making literature and literary influence legitimate in the contemporary novel. Although I think the first novels worthy and larger than they look, I applauded when she expanded her range to men, novels of manners, and finally to global concerns. When others began to call her "trendy," I reveled in how much she knew about the world. I found her references to "yellow ribbons" in *The Ice Age* almost mystical; we were involved in the Iranian debacle when I read it. The woman herself is the kind I admire: she feels quite ordinary but is remarkable.

I wanted my grouping of the novels and short stories to let the reader find Drabble's growth, really the intensification of her themes. Since she is so pursued by the "woman question," I meant to see if she really did nothing with men until driven to in *The Needle's*

Eye, nothing global until *The Ice Age.* To those ends, I have tried to read Drabble's text and let my audience do so.

My ordering has caused some wrenching chronologically, since I have placed Clara, of the fourth novel, with Sarah, of the first, as "young women." Similarly, I delayed the second novel, *The Garrick Year,* until chapter 6 to set the stage for a discussion of Drabble on marriage.

The chapter titles are not limited, as they suggest, to women. Independence (chapter 3) moves beyond Rosamund in *The Millstone* to relate men and women and early and late works. The same is true of "helplessness" in chapter 4, though the focus is on Jane in *The Waterfall,* a book that analysis has taught me to like. The principal "helpless independent" (chapter 5) is Rose of *The Needle's Eye,* but she quickly took me to the general Drabble theme of inequality and, though I present some of them earlier, to Drabble's males, for she shares the role of protagonist with Simon Camish. In chapter 7, middle age links the last three novels and males as well as females. Since Drabble has largely aged with her characters, her achievement as set out in chapter 8 seemed apt as well as obligatory.

I am grateful to Miss Drabble for providing her photograph. I owe thanks also to the following publishers for permission to quote her works: A. D. Peters and Macmillan for "The Gifts of War," "Hassan's Tower," and "The Reunion"; Literistic for "Crossing the Alps" and "A Voyage to Cythera"; *Ms.* for "A Success Story"; Weidenfeld and Nicolson and William Morrow for *A Summer Bird-Cage* and *Jerusalem the Golden;* Random House and Alfred A. Knopf for *The Garrick Year, The Ice Age, The Needle's Eye, The Waterfall, The Middle Ground, The Realms of Gold,* and *A Writer's Britain;* Weidenfeld and Nicolson for the Longman edition of *The Millstone, The Genius of Thomas Hardy,* and *Arnold Bennett: A Biography;* G. P. Putnam's Sons for "A Day in the Life of a Smiling Woman"; and the *Ontario Review* for "Homework." My thanks, too, to the editors of *Critique* for permission to use my article, " 'The Society We Have': The Search for Meaning in Drabble's *The Middle Ground"* (23 [1982]:83–93).

Lynn Veach Sadler

Methodist College

Chronology

1979   *For Queen and Country: Britain in the Victorian Age* and
       A Writer's Britain: Landscape in Literature.

1980   *The Middle Ground.*

Chapter One

Margaret Drabble and the "Writer's Work"

As a result of the many interviews she has given, we know Margaret Drabble perhaps as well as any novelist. She appears a genuinely good human being, one almost too good to be true: never snide, superior, or pretentious; always caring about others. She has been unusually open about her own attitudes and their influence on her work, and a great consonance exists between her life and her writings. She is morally committed to the betterment of the world and its people, yet believes that fate or chance finally determines who is privileged in this life and who is not. Her characters are honest enough, nonetheless, to revel in their privilege. She feels that her own luck is almost uncanny but is simultaneously aware of how hard she works. That kind of paradox laces life as she interprets it and presents it in her novels. It accounts in large measure for their contradictions. Her biography is a veritable women's liberationist exemplum, but she antedates the women's movement and depicts females who are, at worst, stereotypically inept and, at best, flawed in typically human ways. Serious-minded, Drabble seems unable to take herself seriously and frequently escapes into the humorous and the bizarre. Accordingly, the narrator intrudes in the novels to effect a breaking of tone that can be disruptive or refreshing. At the same time, Drabble has spent much of her career consciously trying to atone for having been an initial success by writing about the problems of the college graduate and the backstage wife.

Background, Family, and Early Education

Drabble, known as "Maggie" to her friends, was born on 5 June 1939 in the northern industrial city of Sheffield. Though her family moved about, the area has continued to exert its influence; it provides a link with Arnold Bennett, the novelist and (possibly) distant relative whose biography she has published, and illuminates the

1

personalities of many of her characters. Accepting one's past is a major theme in the novels.

Her father, John Frederick Drabble, is a barrister, a county court judge, and a novelist. She responded to *Who's Who* only because her entry would appear next to his.[1] He and his wife were the first of their families to be graduated from college, and they simply assumed that women should be educated and have jobs (Rozencwajg, 339). Margaret Bloor Drabble was always "convinced" that her daughter would "be something wonderful" and does not believe that she has ever been "fully stretched" (Poland, 26–61). She helps to explain Drabble's empathy with the plight of women. To care for her children, she stopped teaching, except briefly while her husband was away in the Royal Air Force, and has suffered from depression for many years. While Drabble has "never been very good at . . . creating 'good' mothers," she describes her own as "good enough" (Milton, 55–56) and finds her "terribly noble" for not resenting her daughter's "freedom" (Rozencwajg, 339). Mrs. Bennett in *A Summer Bird-Cage* is most like her.

Although the family is Anglican, Drabble and her sisters were sent to a Quaker boarding school for girls, the Mount School in York, and she shows the impact of the Quaker doctrines of the presence of God in every individual (Hardin, 286) and of the equality of all men and women. Her serious approach to literature may stem from this source. She is concerned with the soul, the less fortunate, the interplay of fate and chance, the nature of wisdom, redemption, and the importance of being in touch with one's depths and of doing right rather than seeking enjoyment (Cooper-Clark, 70). Not a churchgoer and never comfortable saying the Creed, she yet believes in loving one's neighbor, enduring unlovely people, and not being solipsistic (Preussner, 575), and so assesses her characters.

An unusual feature in Drabble's novels is their exploration of the world's privileged and lucky, who are different because they have talent, looks, intelligence, health, esteem, and money and, feeling guilty, must prove worth by living difficult, complicated lives. In her view, they have a social conscience and are beset by the Puritan work ethic. She finds them deserving their luck because they worry about whether they deserve the "magnificent hand of cards" "fate" has given them (Hardin, 289) and about those who lack choice and grace. Drabble's interviews reveal the same concerns about her own success and "luck."

The lucky get grace by accepting their privileged lot in life and not fighting their fate. In a prominent image, it "descends like a kind of bird from the sky" (Hardin, 284). But, another paradox, luck is also made by hard work, and Drabble "cannot really believe" in Calvinist election (Hardin, 286). We may be governed by accident and fate, but we must not feel that there is nothing we can do about our lives (Cooper-Clark, 73). We must persist and endure.

Literature has special efficacy for Drabble, who believes that it should always teach about living and values. Ironically, her mother became an atheist by reading George Bernard Shaw (Hardin, 277). Literary allusions abound in her works because, in unprecedented situations, we must ask how a particular author or character would solve a problem (Cooper-Clark, 71).[2] She links her own family to a great literary one: like the Brontës, the Drabble children wrote and performed plays and participated in elaborate games.[3]

Drabble acknowledges writing repeatedly about relations with sisters and parents (Milton, 54), though we learn little about her younger brother and sister. She accepts the influence of her idolized older sister Antonia ("A. S. Byatt"), a scholar and novelist, for both her sibling rivalries and sisterlike soulmates, for example, Clara and Clelia in *Jerusalem the Golden*. This duality helps explain the ambiguity in her novels and her belief that life is contradictory and is constantly shifting from one such extreme to another (Cooper-Clark, 74).

Children and Childhood

Drabble is saccharine when she talks about children. They give her "the greatest pleasure in her life" and have helped to "discipline and organize" her, whereas the childless become "lazier and lazier" (Poland, 257–58). Parental love is an image of God's love and a very pure form of loving that avoids the problems of sexual relationships (Cooper-Clark, 74). A baby makes it impossible to ignore reality and gives one access to the "enormous common store of otherness about other people" (Preussner, 575), themes in *The Millstone* and *The Waterfall*. Contrastingly, as in *The Needle's Eye,* children can limit the lives of their mothers and make them deny themselves. But parents can paralyze their young, too, and, while being a daughter is not much fun, being a mother is "wonderful" (Cooper-Clark, 74). When Drabble interviewed Jane Fonda, they discussed not only

the absence of positive female role models but the problems of being
working mothers.[4]

Drabble has vivid memories of a rather lonely childhood. She
stuttered (does so occasionally now), and her bad chest kept her ill.
She hated games, though she liked swimming and riding and was
"absolutely fascinated" (Milton, 53) by the creatures in Sheffield's
ditches, a love she and Frances of *The Realms of Gold* share. One of
her childhood idols, Boadicea, the British queen who led a revolt
against the Romans, is also shared with Frances. Only when being
intelligent was acceptable, at about age thirteen or fourteen, did
she have many friends.

Marriage

Drabble attended Newnham College, Cambridge, and, although
she received double honors (a "starred first") in English, she describes
her college life as "one long party" (Poland, 257) during which she
did a great deal of very successful acting with her future husband.
She married Clive Walter Swift in June 1960, during graduation
week, and they joined the Royal Shakespeare Company. Everybody
was "very nice" to her, but wives were like "stage furniture." She
understudied Vanessa Redgrave but resented her career going nowhere (Coleman, 23).

Isolated in Stratford, pregnant, bored, and frustrated, Drabble
elected the easiest career for her circumstances—writing. *A Summer
Bird-Cage* (1963) was a success with readers and critics. She wrote
her first three novels while pregnant with Adam Richard George,
Rebecca Margaret, and Joseph (named for the son in *The Garrick
Year*), making them cover the time span of the actual writing, nine
to twelve months. Because she either had to take the children to
the theater or stay at home, she at length felt unable to keep
"everything going" and left the stage to write.

When school time arrived, Drabble gradually stayed more often
in London with the children. "Never particularly practical," Clive
left her most of the family duties. She gave up a job writing television
reviews for the *Daily Mail* because he feared she would hurt friends'
feelings (Rozencwajg, 346). The hiatus came when Drabble received
an English Society of Authors scholarship for travel abroad. Despite
the difficulties of mothering three children from one to six years in
age and having Clive refuse to go to Paris with them because he

was working in a Chichester theater, she was "damned" if she would turn it down (Rozencwajg, 345). They were eventually divorced in 1975, and when he first left, she did not know if she would be able to write again. Later, she nearly sued a magazine that had her say women could write because they could live on their husbands' incomes (Poland, 259). Her novels teem with unhappy marriages and not particularly salutary portraits of the theatrical world. On the other hand, Drabble remained "enchanted" by Clive's family, "so unlike" her own (Hardin, 277).

The Writer at Home and at Work

Drabble lives in a red brick terrace house in Hampstead, North London, close enough in to bicycle to the British Museum to do research. Her living room is bright red, a color that recurs in the interiors described in her works. Her garden abuts the back wall of John Keats's house. She has rarely worked at home because of her children but went to an office in Bloomsbury three days a week except during school holidays.

A "natural" writer, part of her luck, Drabble does not usually revise and finds composition easy—the sentences "pour out." Typically, she begins writing at quarter of ten and works until lunch, occasionally later. She becomes irritable when the writing does not go well (Milton, 51) and wants to entertain and be lucid and readable. She is often cited as summing up the English attitude toward the experimental novel: she will not write one and prefers to be at the end of a dying tradition she admires than at the beginning of one she deplores.[5]

Drabble is modest but self-possessed enough to wear a floppy hat and carry a briefcase and to wonder why critics do not see the humor in her novels. Her interviews reveal her as extraordinarily busy and energetic and as accomplishing an amazing amount while feeling very ordinary: "There must be a lot of people like me" (the title of the Poland interview). If she had not been "lucky" enough to get a publisher forthwith, she would have kept on writing. She contributes regularly to British literary journals, periodicals, and papers; reviews books; writes and broadcasts for the BBC; and conducts interviews with such notables as Doris Lessing. Her reviews appear frequently in the *Listener,* whose literary editor knows what Drabble fancies (e.g., Horace Walpole's correspondence), but she is too hon-

orable to review fiction, a "sort of backbiting territory" (Rozencwajg, 347). She is a joint editor of the *New Stories* series and,
with B. S. Johnson, has edited a group novel, *London Consequences*
(1972). Her concern that literature be a serious illustration of ways
of coping with life is present whether she is reviewing Virginia
Woolf's letters, Doris Lessing's stories, or a biography of Frieda
Lawrence or telling how Katherine Mansfield's short story "Miss
Brill" affected her.

Drabble has written no poetry since the age of fifteen, but she
has authored the plays *Laura,* produced by Granada Television in
1964, and *Bird of Paradise,* performed in London in 1969, and has
written the screenplay *A Touch of Love* (1969) for the movie of *The
Millstone.* She also has taught a course once a week at Morley College
in London and included women novelists. All the while, she continues to read and reread literature with avidity and is revising the
Oxford Companion to English Literature.

In addition to her writing, Drabble participates in worthy causes,
including an annual lecture tour for the British Arts Council during
which she lets children know they do not have to be ashamed of
writing poetry. She served the Home Office in Whitehall Palace as
a panelist examining the British right to privacy laws. Striking a
decidedly women's liberationist note, she says that, when she arrived
"worn out" from all she had already done that day, her colleagues
were still quite fresh (Poland, 260). She has also been in demon-
strations, including one for Dr. Benjamin Spock and one against
the government's Rhodesia policies. When asked if demonstrating
were not the "fashionable," "woman's page thing to do," she responded, with her usual grace and humor (and contradictoriness),
that she is "very much a woman's page writer" (Coleman, 23).
Elsewhere, she admits with the same drollery that she belongs to
"the 'nose-in-the-washing-machine' school of fiction."[6]

The Drabble Canon

Passionately resisting solipsism, Drabble has moved from the
semiautobiographical to a wider and wider canvas. Yet, although
she claims some embarrassment for the early novels, they too were
larger than self. In *A Summer Bird-Cage* (1963), Sarah is struggling
with privilege as well as identity and is far more palatable, if no
more believable, than Anne, her youngest heroine, in "A Pyrrhic

Victory" (1968). Emma (*The Garrick Year*, 1964) accommodates to marriage because of her children and an emergent understanding of limitation generally. In *The Millstone* (1965), independent Rosamund becomes less self-involved through Octavia but remains flawed. Clara of *Jerusalem the Golden* (1967) is the negative role model of acquisitiveness, though her shortcomings are lessened by her youth and background. Another negative exemplar is Jane in *The Waterfall* (1969): talented but helpless, she is "lucky" enough to experience a classic love affair.

Critics often see Drabble's artistic and thematic breakthrough as *The Needle's Eye* (1972). It is a long novel of social concern that ends in compromise with the human situation as Rose, independent but helpless before the odds, denies the pull of the ascetic life she has carved and restores the family as family. The inclusion of a male protagonist is generally viewed as Drabble's declaration that she is not merely a "woman's writer."

But Drabble had already given a superb view from inside Gabriel's head in *Jerusalem the Golden* and sympathetic men in "Hassan's Tower" (1966), "A Voyage to Cythera" (1967), and "Crossing the Alps" (1969). While David causes trouble in *The Realms of Gold* (1975), Anthony becomes the main character in *The Ice Age* (1977). We quickly find that the human perspective, rather than the male or female, is uppermost in the novels. There are awful males (the husband in "A Day in the Life of a Smiling Woman," 1973) and awful females (Meg in "Homework," 1977–78). If no male is ever the equal of Drabble's "golden girl," Frances *(The Realms of Gold)*, even she has very human problems, one of which, middle age, she shares with Anthony of *The Ice Age* and Kate of *The Middle Ground* (1980). Male and female are flawed in "The Reunion" (1968), and Kathie, of "A Success Story" (1972), is as "unsuccessful" as Jenny in "A Day in the Life of a Smiling Woman." *The Needle's Eye* in fact has much more in common with "The Gifts of War" (1970), another exploration of inequality and privilege. They forecast Drabble's maturing interest in human and near-cosmic concerns as finally blazoned forth in *The Ice Age*, the culmination of her worries about such matters as education and India, Africa, and Vietnam (Poland, 264). Afterward she perhaps felt entitled to return to a woman approximately her own age[7] with Kate in *The Middle Ground*.

The critical works reveal similar commitments. Her monograph on Wordsworth (1966) presents that poet's concern for the "unlovely people" of the world, for the diminution of one's powers with age, and for moments of integration, all of which are echoed throughout Drabble's works. Indeed, he, along with John Bunyan, has probably most influenced her thinking. Her biography of Arnold Bennett (1974) shows respect for ordinary people and the reconciliation with one's origins and past that is a constant Drabble theme. In the introduction to *The Genius of Thomas Hardy* (1976), which she edited, Drabble emphasizes universality achieved by focusing on the temporal and ordinary, a fair rendering of her own method. *A Writer's Britain: Landscape in Literature* (1979) is also an apt statement of her aims in its delineation of "every writer's work" as "a record both of himself and of the age in which he lives, as well as of the particular places he describes."[8] As a writer, Margaret Drabble remains true to herself and her experiences and yet remarkably true to the human spirit and condition.

Chapter Two
Young Women

A Summer Bird-Cage

One of the most promising recent graduates of Cambridge, a bored Drabble now found herself waiting backstage at Stratford for her husband and her first child. She remembered having considered Simone de Beauvoir's *The Second Sex* as new territory for fiction and became, with the publication of *A Summer Bird-Cage* in 1963, when she was twenty-four, the first English woman to voice the "delusive promise" of college life.[1] Yet later she was shocked when a group of Cambridge seniors asked her "if it were really so awful" after leaving college (Firchow, 107). Sarah Bennett, Drabble's heroine, is just out of college with highest honors, a "shiny, useless degree" (8), and no career. Unlike Drabble in being single, she does, we eventually learn, have a marriage prospect. The question of what to do with her life is paramount.

Sarah is going home to Warwickshire from Paris where, since she finished at Oxford two months before, she has tutored French girls in English. She will be a bridesmaid for her sister, already two years out of Oxford, who is marrying Stephen Halifax, a wealthy novelist. Her first-person narration seems to offer a simple case of sibling rivalry, with Louise *grand dame* to her *jeune fille* (9–10), plotted about the mystery of this marriage. On its eve, Sarah finds Louise pacing and drinking, more accessible than since they were children.

Only Sarah seems unaware that Louise is in love with John Connell, the actor who is Stephen's best man and who allows Drabble to draw the theatrical world. Retrospectively writing down the story to make sense of it, Sarah reveals the clues that should have alerted her. Not the least is a tableau with Louise before John in a dirty brassiere brushing her hair while he waits for her suitcase.

Sarah assumes herself now free of Louise but begins to be bombarded with news of her and to meet her by chance. Out of curiosity, she accepts a party invitation and gains the insight that Louise has married for money. When she accompanies "Loulou" and John to a pub, their amorousness makes their relationship unmistakable.

Sarah accepts a party invitation from David Vesey, a friend of Francis, whom she will marry when he completes his year at Harvard studying political theory. The novel is not, after all, about her love-hate relationship with Louise. She "had intended to keep herself out of [the narration]," but the danger or unpleasantness in a female's going to a party alone draws her into the open: she is more concerned with making sense of her own life than of Louise's.

Throughout, Sarah claims that she lives at a high-serious level and manufactures difficulty rather than finding easy outs, but the good nature and ease of her narration belie her "bad patch." When Jackie Almond, the "nicest" man at David's party, takes her home, she collapses in tears. Later, missing Francis terribly after watching Louise and John, she calls Jackie for a second try.

Again Louise intrudes. Sarah and Jackie are just settling in when she telephones for help: Stephen has locked her out in her dressing gown after finding her in the bath with John. Jackie leaves; Louise arrives and tells the story of her bad marriage.

Life among the privileged.   *A Summer Bird-Cage* is the story of Sarah's run for independence. Pretty and intelligent, she is privileged and knows that such privilege is given, not earned. She sets the pattern for other Drabble characters by being self-conscious about her luck and simultaneously taking alarm at its unfairness and fearing that it might disappear. She is squeamish because she must add to her cache being "lucky in love." Her uniqueness is that she cannot accept Francis as her due. She manufactures difficulties under the pretense that she is struggling to gain what she already has. The book plays her out like a fish, but we know that she controls this particular line. What she is too young to see is that real difficulties will befall her as life provides its own traps and snares.

Traps and snares.   The title is from John Webster's *The White Devil:* " 'Tis just like a summer bird-cage in a garden: the birds that are without, despair to get in, and the birds that are within despair and are in a consumption for fear they shall never get out" (1.2.42–45). While critics connect the allusion with *domestic* traps and dead ends and most of the bird figures are female (8–9, 21–22, 26, 84, 116), Drabble refuses the consistency of the stereotype. A male figure, Charles Lovell, is also "chirpy" (118). While he and his friends trap Sarah into feeling that everyone else is leading a progressive life (119), she entraps Louise in the stereotype of another bird image. Sarah ignores having seen Louise pacing "like an animal in a small cage trying to take exercise" (22) and interprets her as "way off, wealthy, up in the sky and singing" (25).

Sarah learns about self-entrapment and the mutual culpability of those who stereotype and those who permit themselves to be stereotyped. Her best exemplar is Louise, who is doubly self-entrapped: in the golden cage of glittering London into which her entree is Stephen and in her refusal of John because an actor cannot be taken seriously as genuinely loving her and cannot provide for her. Sarah herself gives way to female dramatics and the stereotype of victimization: she feels "like someone living in a paper house surrounded by predatory creatures" (87). But hers is not the simple world where men are predators and women their victims. She allows Louise to class them with the predators and their frumpy cousin Daphne with the "tame, shabby animals in zoos" (175), though she feels guilty about the labeling and feels more herbivore than carnivore.

Sarah learns that life is not easy, that it refuses to be either this or that. She quickly corrects Smee's dismissal of her as "going to be a don's wife" with "No. I'm going to marry a don" (146), but when he then asks what she will be, the riddle that keeps her "in occasionally panic-stricken effort . . . year in, year out," she responds "I will be what I become. . . ." Male obtuseness is also present in female friendships being "invariably described pejoratively" (76) and in her father's calling sad, tearful Kristin a slut, but Sarah, who thinks the girl's woes more cosmic than homesickness, meets the crisis only with complementary and stereotypical tears. When her favorite cousin, Michael, describes Kristin as "sex-starved" (31), Sarah becomes the "annoyed feminist." Having previously lamented the unfairness of women's being born "with so little defence, like a soft snail without a shell" while men are "defined and enclosed" (29), she attributes Michael's assessment to "all his odious masculine unperplexity" (31). Yet Sarah arrives at her distinction between the sexes by contrasting Louise and herself as brides, and her anger quickly gives way to a wish for the race, not just for females: "I would so like people to be free, and bound together not by need but by love."

Critics read the book as Sarah's year-long study of marriage to see if she wants Francis, and bad marriages abound. Drabble uses the stage technique of foil characters not only for marriage, however, but for ways of coping with life generally. Unmarried women are also negatively presented. Despite her scholarly bent, Sarah, still stereotyping, will not join the female dons because they are spinsters, cannot be sexy, and are badly dressed. Widowed Aunt Betty is everybody's stooge. Sarah admires Simone, Drabble's salute to the androgynous figure of Simone de Beauvoir, and acknowledges her as "the most singular character in the subversive feminine realm which men are so ready to resent and to misunderstand" (75–76) but would only occasionally like to be her and knows she has "the signs of a short term." She dismisses all her role models as she recalls Simone's calling card, a black twig with one "leafless, austere yellow flower" and Stephen and Louise's "dried grasses in long Swedish vases": "Simone, the flower without the foliage, and Gill, the foliage without the flower. I should like to bear leaves and flowers and fruit, I should like the whole world . . ." (75).

One impediment to world-getting is children. Michael's suggestion that Louise will have offspring infuriates Sarah, but when her sister calls, upset about Stephen, Sarah's first thought is that she is pregnant. Gill gets an abortion but is one of the few people really wanting children—but not accidentally and without her consent; she felt the baby a leech sucking her blood (43–44). Ironically, her marriage dissolves when she calls Tony a "foundling." Sarah sides with Gill against smooth-lifed Stephanie, though, and vows that the baby she "might some day bear" will be "born of blood and sweat and tears" or not be hers (94). Hesther Innes becomes her image of motherhood despite the fact that she tried to gas herself because the baby would ruin her career as an actress. Sarah witnesses the beauty-terror of motherhood and is not paralyzed.

The learning process.   For Drabble, writing novels is a means of exploring alternative life-styles, and such exploration is the genesis of Sarah's writing. Her tale of Louise is an extension of her tendency to note people. What she is observing is not just marriage and nonmarriage. Like Louise, she could already be married for money, but the banker's son was too boring. She is learning to reject the emergent extremes and encompass what the extremes miss. She realizes that, because she is not as beautiful as Louise, she has thought of herself as a Daphne. She does not, like Gill (and Drabble) have to marry straight out of college or, like Louise, wait over two years. She is picking her way, somewhere in between, enlarging her own humanness by seeing and accepting the best and the worst in those

around her. Like most humans, Sarah is a paradox. She feels guilty
about having so much, yet is determined to have more. Louise is
her foil. Both sisters want to have their cake and eat it too, but
Louise is the solipsist who will live the life she wants by keeping
love "as a sideline" (215). She has been scared off love as a basis for
marriage by the stereotypical Stella Conroy. Sarah is not soured or
thrown off course no matter how bad or good the examples. She
reacts to the one successfully married couple in the book as "the
sort of people one might very much like to be, if one didn't suspect
that through thus gaining nearly everything one might lose that
tiny, exhilarating possibility of one day miraculously gaining the
whole lot" (92). The problem is their stasis; Sarah changes. As she
waits for Francis, she tests and tries. At the end, she is "waiting
to take up [her] life again, not indeed where [she] left off. . . .
But somewhere, and somewhere further on, moreover" (219).

Sarah would reconcile everything, worries about "who fits where"
(but likes those like Simone who do not fit [51]), and tries to "fix
up an infinitesimal bit of the future" (53), but she will always see
ugly and beautiful, men and women, good women and bad women
as they are, will learn from them what she can, and will be the
stronger for taking both the short and long views. When Louise
shocks her with the "virgin bride" question on the eve of the wedding, Sarah turns the "lamb-to-the-slaughter" image to how awful
it must be for the man to be the slaughterer.

Sarah may fall into the error of stereotyping, but she is not afraid
of stereotypes. She admits that Francis has carried her "around in
his pocket" (79) and is enchanted with being her "love's lovely
angel" (89). She denies that women are justified by marrying but
defends men for liking "silly girls" (84), mocks her own tale as a
"female love-love-love story" (201), and admits "those stupid home
truths about a woman being nothing without a man" (198). She
applies the bird imagery of the title to express not being trapped
by Francis but being trapped without him as the couple in the boat
makes her feel "stagnant and covered in oil and dead feathers" (122).
Complementing this moment are her being "weighted down to
earth" by the thought of Daphne when everyone else is "high up
and laughing" (122) and her sense of chains loosed and burden
lifted, an illustration of Drabble's fondness for John Bunyan, when
she escapes from Louise's party (142).

Sarah also admires the role reversing of Louise, who calls at the theater for John rather than being called for. While she later finds herself wrong to expound on the classic form of Louise's position ("something more deeply rooted in the shapes of life than the eternal triangle of a woman's magazine" [192]), she can put aside her disapproval of Louise to get at a larger dimension. She operates from a high sense of honor as she makes her run for independence and identity, trying to be fair, if not always successfully (e.g., Stephen), to all parties.

Sarah's vocations.   If Sarah were not so enchanting and fetching, she might age into Rose Vassiliou of *The Needle's Eye*. She is very hard on herself, always admitting that she "doesn't know why" (8, 11) and that she has problems with new ideas (21). She likes feeling "tougher" than others (11), has avenged herself against Louise in devious ways, and likes to play the martyr. Prepared to do whatever she must "to gain a sense of hope" (16), she is stoical and "constant only to effort" (172). She does not like to be at home where she gives in to the luxury of having her meals cooked and her bed made. Drabble's Quaker background has permeated Sarah, and her personal vocation becomes trying to find the light within. She admires Gill's mother, a "prison-visiting Quaker" who actually does what she talks about doing and who objects to Tony because of "his total lack of responsibility and social conscience, and his habitual promiscuity" (45).

The Quaker "light within" stands in contrast to the aureate imagery. Ironically, Sarah is taken by Stephen as "an image of the young bright set," "a picturesque illustration of London culture" (170), but Louise is the real symbol of the glittering London bird cage. Quickly she passes the point of "feverish glitter" induced by her leather coat and desires designer clothes that not even Stephen is rich enough to buy. While she can be "dazzling, as though the light were shining through her" (59), more often her shine is pejorative (23, 25), and she remains the Snow Queen. Her last job was in another glittering world, advertising, but she gave it up as getting her nowhere; neither has marrying for money. She will always be driven and dissatisfied.

For Sarah, Paris was not serious enough (8). Her filing job at the BBC helps to pass the days, but if she had married Francis and gone to America to live on his scholarship, they would have faced the same economic problems as Tony and Gill. More important, she would be no further along in the quest for what to do with *her* life. At the end, she is about to "get it all": Francis and a career.

Sarah has become a writer, a career that, as Drabble found, can be combined with a family. She has worked hard on her college essays, the antithesis of Thomas Hobbes's "study-bound" world (61), and disapproves of humorless Stephen the "social satirist" in whose books no one escapes stereotyping. Sarah, on the other hand, will be fair, like Drabble, to the rich and the privileged. While they like the same writers, except Kingsley Amis, he likes them for the wrong reasons. Her ambition is to write a book as good as *Lucky Jim*. We know she is a writer because she uses the same terminology about writing as she used previously about her goals in rebutting Smee: "[Amis] was writing about those people because those were the people he was writing about . . ." (64). She criticizes Stephen for talking "professionally" "whereas these things were life and death" to her (63).

The novel as novel. Although *A Summer Bird-Cage* was immediately successful, Drabble and the critics are generally negative about its form and style, finding it "rambling and desultory" (Rozencwajg, 343). She gives the appearance of control by naming chapters for specific events (e.g., "The Wedding," "The Reception"), and some may react to their surface frivolity. But Drabble has always been praised for her lucidity and fresh, personal style, and the first novel is no exception. It reads easily, is entertaining, and, albeit a bit "cute," fits Sarah. Drabble was daring to adopt a first-person narrator, a technique that often guarantees rejection by a publisher. Also refreshing are the humor (e.g., Louise upset because she is wearing her bath cap when Stephen catches her with John), the turn of phrase ("how lit. critically you put it" [210]), and the upending of literary allusions (Kristin "depressed amongst the alien dishes" [26]).

Drabble uses form as meaning to emphasize the mother-daughter relationship and the theme of ambiguity and doubleness by switching to a dialogue (66–69); Mrs. Bennett *of course* wants Sarah to have a proper career only. . . . Also fetching and effective is the abrupt shift with the arrival of the party invitation when Sarah begins to tell what she had meant to withhold. There is as well an effort to arouse suspense. Sarah responds to John's calling the wedding a farce with the information that she did not find out for months what he meant; when Louise says that she will have her cake and eat it too, Sarah does not see what she meant for "ages" (65). This cliché has the additional value of serving as one of the themes of the book and as a point of contrast between the sisters.

A *Summer Bird-Cage* is a refreshingly off-handed character study of playful/serious Sarah with elements of the novel of initiation as she learns about marrying for money and about infidelity. It is also a thematic and a quest novel. Its major themes are reconciliation with one's lot among the privileged and the avoidance of paralysis in the face of life's inconsistencies and paradoxes. Its quest is Sarah's search for a place for herself that will at the same time let her have Francis. Its achievement is the identity it establishes; we may remember the Bennett sisters of Jane Austen's *Pride and Prejudice* or the older Drabble sisters, but only briefly. We wonder what the Cambridge seniors were so worried about.

Jerusalem the Golden

Jerusalem the Golden (1967) also covers approximately a year and is told retrospectively. For the first time, Drabble uses third-person narration and includes a male point of view (discussed in chapter 5). This character study is tightly controlled and centers on the efforts of the protagonist, Clara Maugham, to escape her origins, northern, industrialized Northam, Yorkshire. Like Sarah, she is trying to decide what to do with her life,[2] but this issue is unresolved. Drabble was twenty-seven when she wrote this fourth novel, which won a James Tait Black Award, but it contains next to her youngest heroine. Clara is twenty-two; Anne, of "A Pyrrhic Victory," is seventeen. In her reactions to her origins, Clara is a cross between Drabble and her mother (Rozencwajg, 335) and has associations with Arnold Bennett.[3] Even so, Drabble deems Clara her "most unsympathetic heroine" and does "not *like* her very much" (Rozencwajg, 338), describing her as "go-head, lively, a grabber"; "She's going to turn into something fearsome . . ." (Hardin, 294, 278).

At age eleven, Clara gets into Battersby Grammar School, where her power over boys and her good grades win her entry into the elite clique. Her adolescent conquests forecast her use of Peter de Salis and Gabriel Denham. Competition becomes her way out, and she wins a state scholarship to Queen's College, London, but remains dissatisfied until, in her last year, she meets the Denhams, who live in a Highgate mansion and are "the real thing" (14). They fulfill the terrestrial paradise—"Jerusalem the Golden"—Clara has imagined through the words of J. M. Neale's hymn in her school days.

When the book opens, Peter has taken her to a poetry reading. She can by now easily recognize his shortcomings, but he does lead her to the Denhams since Mr. Denham, a lawyer, is one of the readers. His daughter Clelia, who is slightly older than Clara and has the same kind of felicitous name, becomes Clara's friend and introduces her to Gabriel. At the end, Clara accompanies him on a business trip using as the excuse for her absence the fact that her mother is ill. They run into Peter Harronson, whom Clara previously met when her French class came to Paris, and attend a party in his aunt's apartment. Exhausted, Gabriel returns to their hotel. She is hurt by his desertion, leaves him asleep, and flies home alone to learn that her mother is dying of cancer. In the standard Drabble mode, Clara feels that she has willed her death by the lie. For the first time, she has a key (literal and figurative) to her mother and her home, but, though she gains insight into Mrs. Maugham, they never make contact. Instead, Gabriel calls and will come for her and drive her back to London.

The Maughams. May Maugham is Drabble's most negative portrait of motherhood, and the Wesleyanism in her background cannot be blamed for her astringency or inconsistency. She terrorizes the neighborhood with her judgments. She is a utilitarian with a passion for useless gadgets. Clara is inured to her harshness and intransigence but not to her inconsistencies. She worries for months about permission to join the school trip to Paris only to have her mother say that she has had a difficult year and deserves a change. Nonetheless, we do not forget that Mrs. Maugham's only Christmas memory is of being urged by her brother to hang up her stocking to be filled with ashes. When Clara learns that she has suppressed her intelligence and will to be happy because of some unexplained death of hope, we judge that life is horrible for most people and that those who escape its horrors are either lucky, like Sarah, or will themselves to escape ("grow by will and strain" [30]), like Clara, and become grasping and drawn to appearance.

One of Clara's brothers has emigrated to Australia; the other, who married a woman "middle-of-the-road" in everything, has subdued his early promise to a job in a chemical factory. Her father worked at the Town Hall at something mathematical, did not like

children, and was killed at a pedestrian crossing when she was
sixteen. Her entire family is afflicted with an "industrial heart" (9),
as Drabble explores the relation between landscape and personality,
one of her constant themes and one brought to fruition in *A Writer's
Britain*.

Clara. What saves Clara is her honesty and the care Drabble
takes to explain why she is as she is. She is driven not only by her
desires for a better life but by an overwhelming sense that she cannot
escape. It erupts in black moments: "connections endure till death
. . . blood is after all blood" (151). Having escaped to Paris with
Gabriel, whose name befits her golden Jerusalem, she relapses into
despair and is chased and pursued and "will never get away, the
apple does not fall far from the tree" (190). Lacking the golden
environment, one has no recourse but experience. Clara becomes a
user because hers reinforces using. Her intelligence brings her first
conquests, the teachers who compete for her when she must choose
between arts and sciences.

The great artistry of the book is that Clara is so much a classic
case and an individual. She is not the stereotypical predatory female;
she does have predatory characteristics. She fears that she likes Gabriel only as her entrée into the world of her dreams and admires
in him "things not personal but generic" (171). Like other Drabble
characters, she finds something sinister about the failure of the fated
moment of recognition; Clelia did not initially impress her, and she
is haunted by the play of the accidental in their meeting.

Clara is another of Drabble's oxymoronic, true-to-life, fated-feel-
ing mixtures. Always willing to work, she studies prior to the poetry
reading and is pleased to find Samuel Wisden the opposite of what
she expected. She will not show her ignorance by asking why Clelia's
mother is famous and accepts her luck in seeing the familiar book
jacket that identifies her as Candida Gray, the novelist. A sponge
and an observer, she picks up all the right phrases but is too modest
to use them. She has never dared buy a drink for herself in a pub
and is so unsure of her taste that she has always worn simple outfits.
She has her first champagne and first flight when she meets the
Denhams and is always diffident about asking the locations of ladies'
rooms. She also frequently surprises herself.

Rigidity. Clara sees anyone not from Northam as a bright blur,
yet its old hymn has prepared her for the aureate world of the
Denhams and for her first escape (Paris), which she invests with the

same imagery: "Narrow was the gate, and the hillsides were crowded with . . . the multitudes, the ranks of the unelect, and she the one white soul flew dangerously forth into some glorious and exclusive shining heaven" (70). She has a mind-set gained by what Northam is not, and no one is there to tell her that golden Paris, with which she becomes disillusioned, foreshadows an equally misleading golden London and golden bosom of the Denhams. To believe so would kill hope. Distrusting appearance is an art for the mature. Yet, under Ash's tutelage, she can see a different Northam and notices herself that, like Rome, it is built on a series of hills. Her rigidity must generally blind her to anything positive in the rigidifying background, however. If it is of Northam, it has to be bad even if it is "shiny." One of her disappointments in Paris is that she has to wear a "shiny" hand-me-down dress, which she mistakes as cheap.

Rigidity makes false gods of complexity and change. In Paris, Clara breaks from the group and looks for adventure. The episode turns out all right but was potentially dangerous. Its success reinforces aberrant behavior as she is joyous, "felt herself to be, at last, living; the thick complexity . . . satisfied something in her that had never before had satisfaction" (82). The need for a "thick" life is addictive to the extent that she becomes not just immoral but amoral. Gabriel's being married entices; she fancies "a complicated, illicit and disastrous love" and has "spent much time gratuitously complicating" "straightforward affairs" "in the hope of discovering the true thick brew of real passion" (133). We must remember that complication for its own sake is a youthful pursuit.

The world of the figurative.   If one's literal is very bad, one retreats to the figurative. Clara takes the world of the Neale hymn, believes in it literally, particularly in its "social joys," and finds it in the Denhams, another example of the Drabble motif of willing or influencing an event by imagining it. As a student of (French) literature, she has not been entirely without critical resources and has thus liked Ash better than the greater catch Higginbotham because he can paraphrase Milton and draw comparisons between a Lone Ranger–like movie and *El Cid*. Starved for the figurative, she is impressed when Ash takes her to a bookstore though she knows that he is out to impress her.

Clara is excited by quotations and clichés, the Bible, hymns, fiction, romances, and advertisements but, at home, is limited to

her grandmother's books stressing the Victorian virtues, to her father's 1895 edition of the *Encyclopedia Britannica,* and to a book of
fables, *The Golden Windows.* Characteristically, in this last, she resists
the story about the boy who realizes that the house of the title is
his own, another example of her rigidity toward Northam. More
appealing is the tale of the two weeds, for, though she can never
decide the winner, the message is the existence of *choice.* If she
cannot be taken in by the unrealistic "cosy adventures of wealthy
children" (37), she proves her worth by instinctively seeking help
in such literature as is available.

   The world of men. Clara appears not only amoral but asexual.
Recognizing men as the power base, she uses them with no feeling
for their being men and as she has used others, notably her teachers.
Though she does not want to be passed off as Gabriel's secretary on
the trip to Paris, she is no feminist. She jettisons Ash when he is
afraid of the cows, vowing not to waste her time going first; she
will get further if she is pulled.

   Try as she will, she cannot like boys. At sixteen, she is not shocked
when Ash tries to undress her, only alarmed because she cannot
respond. When the Italian picks her up in Paris, she sees part of
the Hemingway movie while he fondles her, but she is responsive.
In college, she reads while men try to make love to her and lies
about the reason, pretending that she would lose control if she let
herself think about what they are doing to her.

   Clara is not homosexual and does not, in defiance of the critics,
think of Clelia in such terms. When Ash tells her about homosexuality, she is fascinated but finds the information merely another
example of the world's interesting peculiarities. She responds to the
news that Gabriel's boss is in love with him only as the family
does—as a joke. She likes the ambiguity of his name and is pleased
to think that he must attract men and women equally. Neither she
nor Gabriel is horrified at the thought that he might have been
incestuously attracted to Clelia; both could be very happy in a
ménage à trois with her for the rest of their lives. Clara and Clelia
insist that they do not feel like marrying, but Clara wants finally
to be Gabriel's wife so that her place in the world will be confirmed.

   Brought up in a home where words of endearment and first names
are avoided and there are no visitors and no touching, Clara can
hardly be blamed for becoming unfeeling and applying monetary
images to the intangible: she has affection but "nowhere to spend

it" (64). As a school girl, she learned "that no affection, however oddly won or placed, is laughable or negligible" (43). Men find her more lavish with acts than words (142); she lets Ash unhook her brassiere, for example, after he takes her to the book shop. At least she has the ethic of paying her way.

Clara is not sexually inexperienced, as she lets Gabriel know to set him at ease, and often muses about what her mother would think if she knew Clara was naked (or drunk [143]). Yet she has never kissed, only been kissed, as Magnus, Gabriel's older brother, makes her realize. She is, as she has said to Gabriel, "too full of will to love" (191), another of the costs of being deprived and of overcompensating by grasping and climbing. An unattractive child, she has willed herself to become a beauty and can never accept her graces as anything other than a means to some desired but unspecified end. Struggle takes its toll. She has most in common with Simon Camish of *The Needle's Eye,* whose ability to feel has also been eroded.

Phillipa Denham. We can understand what has molded Clara, but Gabriel's wife remains an enigma. Some may see Phillipa as the product of a world in which women are second-class citizens and the masses are oppressed, but she is another of the novel's reminders that appearances can be deceiving, and her brutalization is not her husband's fault. Clara perceives her as "capable of contending with anything" (137) and as straight off the front page of *Harper's.* Remote and bored, she seems an extension of the golden world as she sits in the Denham drawing room "irradiated from behind by some small gold local source of light" (146).

Aside from a resentment of her in-laws, it is difficult to say what is wrong with Phillipa. Whatever she is, she is an original. She refuses to cut up food, and so her children refuse to eat anything but baked beans. Yet the kitchen is her only impressive room, and Gabriel buys another gadget for her while he is waiting for Clara in Liberty's. Her problems date from the second week of the marriage when he found her crouched in the dark crying over birth control. Since then she, like Kristin in *A Summer Bird-Cage* and Stephen in *The Realms of Gold,* has been assailed by a kind of cosmic grief. Hers was relieved only in childbirth—until her third child was a girl and all of "her wounds" were thus "reborn" (166). We get what we get from Gabriel; Phillipa keeps herself to herself and intrigues Drabble enough to pursue her and her type further.

The Denhams and Clara.   The Denham Jerusalem is not the
London bird cage, but it is not perfect. Drabble's contribution to
the contemporary novel is not the "dispossessed [who] shall forever
meet at street corners, forever divulging to useless auditors their
need" (169), but the privileged. The Denhams have culture, beauty,
tradition, love (for one another and for others), and the "custom
and ceremony" that form the title of the one book by Candida that
Clara has read. But they are not impervious to the ambiguities of
existence that Drabble delineates, as Candida's latest novel, *A Fall
from Grace,* indicates. Golden, the Denhams are not for this world
and, consequently, can maintain themselves only so long as they
do not let in reality.

The mother is too good, too successful, and yet is the "archetypal
victim" (119) of her own goodness. She has had five offspring and
a magnificent career, but children are driving most of her children
mad. The oldest daughter goes crazy when she leaves the "golden
nest." Magnus is not appreciated because he works too hard and is
clever rather than "strange and wonderful" (196). A rebel like Ame-
lia, he loves Phillipa, envies Gabriel, and moves in on Clara. Gabriel
steals food on his frequent visits home and knows that anyone with
three children will always be poor. His own separate him light years
from Clara, invade his dreams when he is in Paris with her, and
eventually force him to sell his soul to television to send them to
Eton. Clelia, who has never said a boring word in her life, seems
a match for Candida but is a frustrated sculptor and talented artist
whose life has come down to reading novels while she tends the art
shop and baby of Martin after his wife runs off. She artificially
remakes herself into an unmarried mother as if to return for answers
to the "prolonged nursery associations" (107) of the room in which
she was once so complete. Annunciata, the youngest, is Clelia all
over again; she might be her own person yet. The others will not;
they are only *Denhams.*

Like Phillipa, the Denhams are wonderfully original. We are not
even allowed to hate Candida's perfection, for while Martin is at
least as interested in the mother as in Clelia, Mr. Denham has a
gleam in his eye for Clara. Her portrait is also shot through with
humor and excuses for others. She may be the epitome of motherhood, the famous novelist posing with her children in their Hesther
Laprade clothes and carrying on the grand tradition by clothing her
children in a christening gown made by her own grandmother, but

when she appropriates James, Martin's baby, a "consolation prize" for her "change of life" (116), he wets all over her review copy of Fanny Burney! She labels children "wonderful excuses for not having done other things" (117), a charge of which she can never be guilty, and admits that she has failed as a teacher because she was afraid of boring her students.

Clara will not end so abominably as Drabble fears. She knows that she is "drawn unquestionably to the appearance of things" (103); she shies from cheating the state by taking a teaching certificate without meaning to teach; and she has crises of meaning when Gabriel leaves her at the party in Paris, when she finds her mother's notebook, and when she talks to him on the phone. Her growth is measured in this last simple instance. Heretofore she has eschewed and feared telephones. Now in the place where she learned discomfiture, she is honest with Gabriel and ready to move on again, if on a diminished plane. Her summum bonum is still a "bright and peopled world, thick with starry inhabitants" (236), but we cannot overlook "peopled" or the denial of stasis that follows: "an eternal vast incessant rearrangement." They are at least the beginnings of antirigidity and antisolipsism. Nor should we miss the fact that Clara, whose name means the "light" she has chased, in her still youthful exuberance here, lifts the leaden weights from Gabriel and lets him free, momentarily, "to ride together, forever ride, as Browning said" (234).

"A Pyrrhic Victory"

The 1968 short story "A Pyrrhic Victory" has Drabble's youngest heroine, seventeen-year-old Anne, and she is also trying to find out who she is or get control of her "loop-holes." Yet the nature of that quest makes the story a near-parody of a later novel, *The Needle's Eye,* and Anne a near-parody of what has become the Drabble person. The tenor is life's both self-made and innate difficulty, and the dominant image is the Bunyanesque hill-to-be-climbed.

Anne and three acquaintances are on a jaunt to Elba. After a night of drinking that has included her first sexual experience, they are doggedly climbing a hill for a picnic. Even when they reach the top, no one, particularly Anne, who feels that she is the least sophisticated, will suggest stopping for lunch. She instinctively knows that, like the typical Drabble person, she will spend her life putting herself into difficulties and intolerable situations. Johnny, the American, on the other hand, simply says that he is hungry, again proving his "authenticity," the mode of being Anne finds so elusive. Her act of self-assertion, throwing their sardine can into a picture-postcard pool, is crude and adolescent and is the Pyrrhic victory of the title. Like Napoleon's triumphs, an analogy Anne imposes, it costs too much. Drabble people, young like Anne or older like Rose in *The Needle's Eye,* make every moment, little or big, a difficulty to be surmounted.

Chapter Three
Independent Women
The Millstone

Drabble was in her third pregnancy when she wrote her third novel, which she used to cheer herself up by remembering her delight in her first child. Though sometimes compared unfavorably with Lynne Reid Banks's *The L-Shaped Room,* *The Millstone* (1965) has been among her most popular novels and was made into a movie, *A Touch of Love,* starring Sandy Dennis, for which Drabble wrote the script. She called the American edition (1969) *Thank You All Very Much* after a line in the film. Although the movie was not well received, the novel won the Llewellyn Rhys Memorial Prize in 1966. It has been translated more often and has received more letters than her other novels, has been adapted for a Swedish women's magazine,[1] and has been compared with her book on Wordsworth.[2] More amazing for the story of an unwed mother who keeps her child, it was published in a casebook for English schools.

Just out of Cambridge, Rosamund Stacey, with the assistance of Hamish Andrews, determines to jettison her virginity but is foiled when she signs her own last name on the hotel register. Attractive to and attracted to men, despite her difficulties with sex, she concocts a way to enjoy their companionship while she works for her doctorate. For a year, she goes with Joe Hurt and Roger Henderson, holding each at sexual bay by letting him think she is sleeping with the other. Fate abhors her abstention, and, after she quarrels with Joe one evening, George Matthews, a casual acquaintance, walks her home, and they make love. Her pride and his diffidence subsequently prevent further contact, though she thinks of him and listens to him on the BBC. Several months later, while she is in the British Museum working on Sir Walter Raleigh, she realizes she is pregnant. She bungles the abortion she attempts with gin and hot water and decides to keep the baby when her older sister advises putting it up for adoption.

Everything falls miraculously into place. Rosamund's parents, ignorant of the crisis, go to Africa for a year and give her their posh flat, which she shares with her arty novelist friend, Lydia Reynolds. Her dissertation proceeds apace, and her only difficulty is with the National Health Service and Pre-natal Clinic. The birth is easy; the child, Octavia, is beautiful. The doctor reveals her situation to her parents, who move on to India. Lydia is not angry when Octavia chews up some of the manuscript of her latest novel, only relieved because Rosamund pretends not to know she and the baby are its subjects. All continues idyllic until a doctor treating Octavia's cold discovers a heart defect requiring a dangerous operation. The child survives, but Rosamund has to have hysterics to get into the ward to see her. Her career is also inordinately successful, and she will soon take a position at a new university.

On Christmas Eve, Rosamund meets George in a chemist's shop, and he walks her home. She lies about Octavia's age so that he can have no idea of his paternity. He tells her he may be going abroad. They have wanted to move toward each other but could not, finally, break the stalemate.

Drabble on and in *The Millstone*. Drabble is bored and "slightly fed up" with *The Millstone* (Milton, 60), is repelled by its "tidiness" and lack of the "extra mess" in her later novels, and was horrified when it was interpreted as a warning not to let one's children play with just anybody (Myer, [37], [19]). In her introduction, she denies that Octavia's illegitimacy was her main interest; rather, she wanted to communicate the experience of childbirth, the importance of a child, the feelings one has for it, and the changes it brings to one's life. She deliberately removed such intervening elements as husband and home and made Rosamund a single, "modern girl" who cannot go to her parents and friends with her problems. While feminists can appreciate the novel, Drabble sees Rosamund as a human; people, not just women, have defects, and hers is "dryness of spirit" (Cooper-Clark, 72).

Paradox plays throughout the book. Rosamund mixes confidence, cowardice, and female stereotyping as she "weep[s] daily for some cause or other" (118). One of the major points is that independence is double-edged—a virtue but an impediment because it separates people. Similarly, the baby is a contradiction. Her coming is "disagreeable, humiliating, painful, and frightening," and, a true "millstone," she will alter Rosamund's life irrevocably, but the experience is also important and rewarding. The bad luck of getting pregnant during one bout of sex becomes good luck because, through the child, named for feminist Octavia Hill, she experiences real love and becomes more human. At play also are the questions of how one can be independent and have others dependent; how one avoids becoming dependent on that dependence; and how one with looks, intelligence, and luck can be lonely.

The book is not so different as it sounds. Rosamund is much like other Drabble heroines, emotionally flawed and struggling to be both a woman and a human. The check-list atmosphere and glibness put off the initiated reader, who grimaces at such standard Drabble fare as Voltaire's admonition to "cultivate one's garden," Bunyan, Freud, a year's "grace," and "the beauty of fate itself" (154). On the other hand, Rosamund's petulance at seeing no way to take the baby-sitter off her income tax anticipates Drabble's restlessness to move to general concerns.

Rigidity. We also admire Drabble's ability to paint the same universal (not to be rigid) with two such different particulars as Rosamund and Clara Maugham, both of whom cast blame on their backgrounds and upbringings. Rosamund reports that her parents, ideological Socialists and Fabians, let her get a Cockney accent associating with working-class children and had the char lady to dine, suffering in silence when she stole the silver. Comfort is dangerous to the soul, and they look for ways to punish themselves for their successes. Dr. Stacey is an economics professor who helps underdeveloped nations but thinks little about dragging his wife with him. Their anticapitalist consciences will not permit them to sublease their flat, so they let Rosamund move in. She in turn cannot bring herself to charge rent or hire domestic help. She knows that her life is too pleasant and "that one ought to do something, preferably something unpleasant, for others" (47), so she tutors— only to turn out to be a very good teacher.

Mrs. Stacey, a feminist, reared her daughters to be equal and make their way. Rosamund considers this educational experiment disastrous. Her older sister, with whom she gets along well enough "as sisters go," majored in economics but married at graduation. Named for a famous woman, Beatrice, Rosamund infers, must be unhappy about wasting her degree. Worse, although Beatrice is the family's only confirmed pacifist, she now lives with her scientist husband near a nuclear station and watches her sons play with guns.

Rosamund has fared little better. She feels that her parents consider
her a dilettante for choosing literature and then eschewing the
"weighty" (e.g., the nineteenth-century novel) for the Elizabethan
sonnets, which lack "moral worth." She is surprised when George
points out that they must be very proud of her, and while they see
the Elizabethans as creative, Rosamund deems them dry.

Staceys are bred to "suffer fools gladly," but Rosamund breaks
the mold in a way that becomes not less but more rigid. She is
despicable when she talks about her brother and sister-in-law. Andrew married a "ghastly girl," and they spend their time having
"worthless" people to dinner and playing bridge. Anyone who goes
to beauty parlors has nothing better to do with her time. . . .
Rosamund's slap at hospitality is a self-indictment. She misses the
play on words in her "poor Clare," for the order of nuns known as
"Poor Clares" has charity. She gets her comeuppance when, after
her difficulties with breast-feeding, she assumes Clare's mania for
cleanliness.

Escaping our backgrounds may be impossible, as Rosamund and
Clara feel, because we take their pattern or rebel, often forcing our
own natures against the grain. Rosamund displays both tendencies
in her choice of men. Joe is the kind her liberal parents must defend.
He is ugly and has the "permanent greyness" (152) of poverty in
contrast to Rosamund's "hard fit shine of the well-nurtured." His
last name, Hurt, casts him forever onto the Staceys' "hard damp
shore of sociological pity." His mechanically pouring out mechanical
novels ought to alert Rosamund to the danger signals at the root
of her choosing him. Roger, on the other hand, represents the world
her parents condemn. He is a wealthy, well-descended Tory barrister
with charm and smooth skin, who will not walk anywhere and is
uncivil to waiters. Yet she has to tell Joe she is pregnant while
Roger guesses. Joe, who is married, will lend her money for an
abortion; Roger offers marriage and a quick divorce, if she desires
it, no matter what the consequences for his career.

Rosamund ought to be gleaning a kinder interdiction: not to be
unyielding and not to stereotype when seeking true independence.
She assumes that she does not fear George because he is "queer," a
predisposition she has inferred from his "camp" jokes. He refuses
to yield to her inspection or take her into his confidence, and she
is accustomed to being secretive and having others reveal all to her.
She has never been able to place him but suspects him less refined

than he appears. Pride, part of the burden John Bunyan's Christian sheds, makes her avoid George's locale, which takes on "a fearful moral significance: it became a map of my weaknesses and my strengths, a landscape full of petty sloughs and pitfalls, like the one which Bunyan traversed" (30). Yet she misses Bunyan's message: there is a world unsusceptible to private charting.

For all her brightness, Rosamund uses knowledge to restrict rather than expand meaning. She attempts to measure events in others' dicta. When her daughter is threatened, she passes fitfully from the immortality of the soul to there being no pain without purpose to justice demanding death for her sin and to the laws of chance. She relies on the aphoristic ("nothing fails like failure" [3]); when Lydia and Joe part, she congratulates herself on knowing that friendship outlives passionate love. She can be cute—"I don't believe in principle, I believe in instinct, on principle" (112–13). She ends little wiser, still blaming her parents for her "inability to see anything in human terms of like and dislike, love and hate: but only in terms of justice, guilt and innocence" (81).

Like other Drabble characters, Rosamund believes that what we think, we get. Thus the sexless year with Hamish molded her ways with all men. Symbolically, the curtain ring she wore to the hotel is donned again, when she is pregnant, to save the feelings of the minister. Her problems are not her fault: "I did not know that a pattern forms before we are aware of it, and that what we think we make becomes a rigid prison making us. In ignorance and innocence I built my own confines, and by the time I was old enough to know what I had done, there was no longer time to undo it" (3). True to character, then, Rosamund, who considers herself in every way superior to Lydia, makes food "edible" while her friend makes it "amazing, rich, and rare." Rosamund can be "fair but not generous" and wants people to stay in their prescribed places (155). At the last, she tells George that her nature is to worry—"There's nothing I can do about my nature, is there?"

Literature in *The Millstone*. Also rigid about literature, Rosamund often misuses it. She takes without loosing its restorative and enlarging powers. When Octavia damages Lydia's novel, Rosamund is too honorable to lie, but she soothes herself with John Stuart Mill's maid burning the only manuscript of Thomas Carlyle's *History of the French Revolution*. She reduces the "modern novel" to the illegality of leaving children unattended after dark (157) while

Drabble wants her to see the revelation of "possibility" through literature. When Rosamund asks a neighbor to watch Octavia while she goes to the chemist's, a vista of communication opens up, and, though she reduces it to people's liking to have others in their debt, she is rewarded by the chance meeting with George. She has another brief moment of insight in realizing that she repeats Ben Jonson's "sin" of loving his son too much.

Rosamund misses out on Lydia's novel as a rare opportunity to see herself as others see her. She does not question her own assessment of Rosamund Stacey, only Lydia's, and remains spiritually crippled by being unable to open herself to others. The failure to communicate with Lydia may not be very important, but the same failure with George has lifelong consequences. By relegating herself to the position of "one of those [George Bernard] Shaw women who wants children but no husband" (105), she not only settles for less and diminishes the literary type—she lies; she does want to marry George.

One of Rosamund's oddities is her inability to discriminate among literature. While we can salute her eclecticism and tolerance, much of what she knows about life, including abortions, comes from "cheap fiction" (1, 3), and given her profession, we wonder why she has read so much of it. In one page of her tale (14), she relates her "virtuous reluctance" to lose her virginity to "every woman's magazine" and offers a variation on Hawthorne: her scarlet letter is for abstinence, not adultery.

Rosamund also manifests confusion about the origins and motivations of literature. Well acquainted with the creative writing world through her friends, she is quite sure that hers is the Aristotelian rather than the Platonic view of fact and fiction (145), that literature is grounded in the real rather than the imagined or ideal. Yet she is surprised that its bons mots sometimes speak the truth (125). She becomes angry when Daniel Defoe's *Journal of the Plague Year* turns out to be fiction. Contradictorily, she is upset with Lydia for basing her novel in "fact," Rosamund's life. The distancing she knows to be necessary to literature could teach her the possibility of maintaining one's independence and making connections. For example, at the Pre-Natal Clinic, a mother suddenly thrusts her baby to Rosamund to hold, and it wets her. Though the episode impresses her, she cannot share it because it is not in a "state fit for anecdote" (69).

Lydia had rather write *bad* books than not write. At twenty-six, having already published two novels, she thinks she has dried up. She has to drag words out of herself like a dirty spider, so she resorts to spinning her web from Rosamund, who misses one of the reasons Lydia takes up with Joe—to find out if he really is the father and put his story in her book. Similarly, Joe wants Rosamund to remember exactly what Lydia says about her chewed-up manuscript so he can "use it some day" (150) in a book. To help her over her block, Lydia creates literature from life whereas she has earlier discarded her own pregnancy as "far too unrealistic for [her] kind of novel" (62). Refused an abortion, she went outside the doctor's office to be knocked down by a bus and lose the baby. Using literature to judge that the tale is not literary, she discards it because it sounds too much like Thomas Hardy's *Life's Little Ironies*. Accidentally, she quotes Wordsworth, the poet of "real life," as she shunts Hardy aside.

Rosamund, on the contrary, believes that because something happens, it is true and is moved by such real-life ironies as being killed while adjusting a seat belt (63). She knows that, had she not been pregnant, she would have broken her neck when she slipped on the stairs after a party, but we get no suggestion that she has gleaned her sense of irony while writing about Michael Drayton's use of it. Literature never is "life and death" to her.

The ultimate irony is that Rosamund remains unaware of the genre of her own story. She writes about Samuel Daniel and knows his "Complaint of Rosamund" but does not realize she has produced her own complaint and not merely one about love gone wrong. Daniel's poem is also "mirror literature": here but for the grace of God and self-determination go you. Privileged Rosamund would be shocked and hurt to realize that she exemplifies what not to do. She does not die, like Daniel's heroine, for the love of a man. Rather, her solipsism dies a little as self-love is replaced to a large degree by maternal love, but she does not come right fully. Her limitations are replaced, if replaced, in most instances by new limitations, and they seem willfully chosen. Like the mother in "The Gifts of War," she knows, for example, that she will someday be left "in darkness" by her child. Why after such recognition does she not enlarge her emotional world? We wonder if the main resonance in "Rosamund Stacey" is not from the last name, a play on "stasis."

The dim life.   The world of Drabble's privileged is not airy.
They are self-denying and self-reliant and believe in the work ethic.
They never enjoy themselves fully because they feel for others, try
to spare their feelings, suffer guilt, and fear they will lose what they
have because they do not deserve it. If nothing can be done about
the inequality of beauty and brains in the world, "that's no reason
why we shouldn't try to do something about economics, is it?" (82).
Rosamund shares this atmosphere. She is not used to happiness,
only to momentary feelings of satisfaction, triumph, excitement, or
exhilaration (101). When she first holds Octavia, the delight is so
great she automatically knows to ration it. Joe is wrong to credit
her pleasure to her being female and yearning for fulfillment through
a child. Rather, through Octavia and for the moment, she ceases
to gnaw at herself about being privileged. Her privileged status
allows her to get by with being an unwed mother in the first place.

The privileged are also lonely. Isolated as a child by intellect and
family status, Rosamund has always fantasized about having a salon
and hates being alone. Her stay in the hospital is cheerful and
sociable, though she satirizes Women A, B, and C for their trivi-
alities. One of the milestones of her life occurred when she and
Beatrice played with two boys in the park until they discovered the
maid and thought them rich: "An hour like that in a lifetime is
quite as much as one can expect" (84).

The world after the birth of Octavia is dimmer. Characteristically,
Rosamund sees as negative the connections it induces with others.
In the Pre-Natal Clinic, she is "trapped in a human limit for the
first time" (55). Rosamund has heretofore seen a world governed
by free will and choice (64) in which love is related to merit and
beauty and one pays a fair price for what one gets. Her own com-
modities are witty conversation, inherited prestige, parties, and
good legs (66). Now, against her nature, she is going to have to
ask strangers for help (69) and, because of Octavia's heart condition,
is in for a lifetime of "checks and examinations" (140).

The gains.   Rosamund makes gains, though we have difficulty
believing she now feels for others in her heart whereas, prior to
Octavia, she felt for them in theory only (66). Her model is a woman
and mother, but the message is still primarily human rather than
female. This woman has fought for the right to see her hospitalized
child and has stopped making excuses for others and pretending
everything is all right to save their feelings (139). She has found

independence—a middle course between solipsism and self-effacement. To Rosamund, who as a child endured any discomfort rather than cause offense, the woman is a revelation.

The view of that woman "thus gently put forward as the result of sad necessity" places in perspective earlier events associated with Octavia, the first when Rosamund is in labor. The voices of the nurses outside her room talking about boyfriends and difficult births come to her "very clearly and purely, the syntax and connections of their dialogue illuminated by a strange pale warm light" (97). Their social bond excludes Rosamund as, symbolically, her pain, eased by medicine, is "no longer personal and therefore bearable." The scene recalls Bunyan's encounter in *Grace Abounding* with the poor women of Bedford sitting in the sun talking about a "new birth" and the insufficiency of righteousness. Bunyan is being reborn in Christ; Rosamund, through Octavia, is supposed to reach a new sense of self and of the self's relation to others, not just her child. Whereas Octavia causes her to say that life will never again be a "simple question of self-denial," we say that it never should have been.

The potential for further growth is underscored as Rosamund aligns herself with the woman in the children's ward by yelling at the nurses and having the hysterics that gain access to Octavia. She also sees that she can abandon rigidity when Octavia's need for food runs counter to the intervals dictated by the authority on child care. Yet she is the old Rosamund in her self-congratulatory comparison of herself to Job.

Again, strain costs. At the end of the novel, still in her mid-twenties, Rosamund has lost weight and has graying hair. She is a very successful university don, a gain that, given her natural endowments, was hers anyway. She is a less successful mother, for, as Drabble tells us in her introduction to the novel, she may love too much for Octavia's best interests. In human terms, she has made small advances, but they have been largely enforced and situational. She may no longer be capable of coolly evolving systems that are fair to others "with the maximum possible benefit" to herself (15), but she has not mastered the art of, has not even begun to see the necessity for, that delicate merging of being one's self, being a self for others, and letting others be there for oneself—true independence. Her distancing, what she would call her "independence," from her family is relived in her willful division from George.

The novel as novel. Rosamund's response to a friend's book summarizes the technique of *The Millstone* and of Drabble's novels generally: "I do not care very much for plots myself, but I do like to have a sequence of events" (8). It spills forth facilely, looks back to details already mentioned, and seems to operate through Drabble staples: "[George] was myself, the self that but for accident, but for fate, but for chance, but for womanhood, I would still have been." Events and episodes stand out: the would-be abortion, the Pre-Natal Clinic so admired by critics, the birth, the fit of hysterics, Octavia's destruction of Lydia's novel, and the Christmas Eve meeting with George. Tightly constructed and easily summed, it is the only novel whose ending Drabble knew when she started (Myer, [37]). Its world is her usual real one of Aquascutum macintoshes, gold lurex jerseys, Viyella nighties, and London streets and buildings.

The Millstone is a study of a character privileged beyond most of us, yet for whom life is a puzzle. If episodic, the episodes are also epiphanic as in the glowing scene with the nurses. They are revelatory for us if not for Rosamund despite her being a successful literary critic accustomed to searching the text for resonances of meaning. Soon, she is going to apply her skill to the everyday and thus let literature teach her about life and its values. She has already found a balance between and a keen delight in working on her dissertation and solving literal puzzles.

Drabble makes limited but striking use of symbolism. Rosamund dreams of these puzzles, of "small blue irregular shapes composing the cloak of the Virgin Mary" (89), and we make the connection between her case as near-virgin mother and the tableau of Rosamund-George-Octavia/Mary-Joseph-the babe on Christmas Eve.[3] If her configuration does have something in common with that other, why can she not see it as right? Likewise, Rosamund merely reports the "tank of tropical fish, surrounded by a circular bench" and her watching them "endlessly and soothingly drifting around their glass cage" (161). She wonders if fish sleep, not about any relationship between their entrapment and her own. Yet the image works in her subconscious, and she later echoes it in the apartment with George: "If one of us did not move towards the other, then we could only move apart. Like two fish, embalmed in the living frozen river, we eyed each other in silence through the solid resistant intervening air, and did not move" (168). Possibility or only stasis? The progress Rosamund has made with those beyond Octavia is merely the reversal of an extreme. She and George had a "sense of touch without contact" (27); now they have contact but no touch.

Other Quests for Independence

Len and Maureen in *The Ice Age*. In *The Ice Age,* the two most successful, independent characters are minor. Len Wincobank and Maureen Kirby, like Clara Maugham, are from the north of England but do not hate it. Len's development of its town centers expresses Drabble's pleased surprise at the changes she found on her return to Sheffield, which Len visits. The northern landscape teaches him his love of grandeur and his dislike of buildings out of scale with their setting.

Anthony Keating, the protagonist, admires Len because he is self-made and combines zeal and carefulness. He knows both sides of arguments, loves and believes in his work and his buildings, and is determined to make others like them. In prison he demonstrates how an energetic person survives an end to purpose. He is his own man without abrasively forcing his way against and over others. He refuses to let Maureen's picture be gawked at but throws a sop by placing a nude portrait in his cell. He is both a man of vision and one who refuses fantasies unless he can convert them to realities. He can empathize, understanding the older prisoners' feeling of being better off inside and pitying the actors reduced to performing in a prison. He communicates with Callander, who cannot be left to "twitch grayly" (182). Despite his origins, he does not suffer from provincialism and chauvinism. He can criticize England, love her history, and admire American architecture. He participates in Drabble's sense of life's possibilities. He does not waste his time in prison but works out in his head his next project. Len appraises and learns from what is going on around him, surprising himself by wondering about the fate of the trees in the greenhouse and being touched by their ability to survive. He believes that he cares more for buildings than people, but his actions belie him. His refrain that one cannot make omelets without breaking eggs aligns him with the woman Rosamund meets in the hospital. Someone must get hurt if progress is made, and Len's works give if they also take away. He can turn a bomb site into a department store and feel sorry for Anthony and shore up his life. Len can face his culpability for the fate of the Aunt Evies of the world and not be paralyzed.

Len knows that his identity needs "dilution rather than reinforce-
ment" (250) but also recognizes that he could not cope if he were
stranded in a foreign town like Alison Murray. Neither is he a
surface person. He cannot share the story of his best meal because
the episode was too much of paradise to bear telling even to a friend.
When he sees Callander going crazy, he does not tell on him or
abandon him, but reassesses himself. Neither does he succumb to
coincidence and chance as explanations for their punishment. He
blames himself when frustration with Callander causes him to lose
his remission; he is glad he took some action and is shocked at
himself for being soothed by the warden's promises. The worst is
not the loss of his pardon but the comment on the human situation:
"He found the idea of going through a bad patch, like everyone
else, inexpressibly dreary. He had thought himself different. He
had made himself different" (251). He remains irrepressible and
resilient and, despite his incarceration, is more independent of circumstance than the main characters.

Maureen is an easy person for women and men to be around. She
starts as a hairdresser but sees the dead end and takes a secretarial
course. Her boss fulfills her expectations of groping, which she does
not mind; she simply realizes she can get someone better. She has
a much healthier attitude toward sex than her Drabble sisters and
enjoys it. Like Len, she can learn from everything, and Flood's
vulgarities help to "refine" her.

Maureen also stands up for other women and will not let Derek
blame his wife. Her mimicry of "my wife doesn't *understand* me"
lets him "get into bed with her with some decent sense of equality"
(248). Alison, so much above her in class, admires her, as does
Anthony, and seeks her advice and sympathy. She finds her, as
everyone seems to, "unthreatening and unthreatened" (257), at ease
with what she is. When Len wants to make her his partner, she
refuses; they enjoy acting out variations on the boss-secretary
relationship.

Like Len, Maureen can self-analyze. She knows she will not remain
faithful while he serves his time and hopes not to be shabby and
give in too soon. When she does fall, she feels relief not only at
being back on sex but at no longer having to pretend to be what
she is not. She also accepts that she may be a bit of a crook like
the others involved in the property scheme.

Maureen's clichés do not grate like Rosamund's. The difference
in their education is one factor, but our acceptance is also related
to her being self-made. She has not had to manufacture difficulty;
neither has she been ravaged by strain and struggle. She and Len
have led an exciting life "nice while it lasted," and it was nice to
see "how the other half lives," but they "got ideas above [their]
station" (262) and lost their hold on reality. It may be her failure
of will that sentenced him, for a "good woman" can keep her man
out of jail. Love will move mountains (260), only not for her. She
has earned the right to these clichés, for she still wakes up in a
panic at 3:00 AM and has spots on her chest from anxiety. Unlike
Len, she has no difficulty with her common humanity and soothes
Alison's fears for Anthony by discussing how people react to stress.

Drabble considers Maureen the "nicest" character in *The Ice Age*.
She writes Len careful letters free of recriminations, and her sojourn
in the high life has not embittered her toward Sheffield, where she
has removed to a shabby flat. She continues to think of herself as
lucky; if she had let Len make her a partner, she would be in jail.
She goes to her mum's on Christmas Eve, though she lets us see
the perspective she has gained not only by recognizing the crowd-
edness but by assessing the occasion positively as a "whole event."
She also takes the larger view, wondering if the good days will come
again for individuals or for the country. When she marries Derek
and they end up the subject of a sociologist's report on the "successful
combination of careers," she finds the time to give interviews "as
a representative of the new world of businesswomen" (265). Maureen
has always been herself and helped others.

Kathie in "A Success Story." Drabble published "A Success
Story" in two feminist magazines (1972–74), and the heroine, Kathie Jones, seems independent. She is a well-known playwright, in
her early thirties, who is modest, works hard, lives with Dan, is
childless but thinks constantly about her own childhood, and is
good "at all the things" that have held women back.[4] Before we
get the salting of "very nicely," we know something is amiss from
the ironic, deprecating opening in which the omniscient narrator
says that this story about a woman could not have been told "perhaps
even five years ago." Does she mean that there were no female
success stories then or that the tale of an independent woman with
Kathie's "flaws" could not have been told earlier when women were
still trying to be Superwoman?

Kathie is familiar territory. She has fought her background, which is between lower-middle and working class (52) and so could not be used for "shock value," has come from another Midlands grammar school, does not quite know the social amenities or the dress code, and is still nervous about parties. Because she was a plain child, she has no confidence in her appearance and has survived through her imagination. Now she is going to a party to meet Howard Jago, the hero of her childhood dreams, and analyzes why she has turned down other opportunities to do so. He has asked to see her, but she is put off by his being a womanizer. She gladly sees him fall prey to a siren at the party and feels some regret at the shock she would have felt at sixteen not to talk with him about his themes.

When Jago flees with Kathie to his place for a nightcap, she refuses to be seduced, and they kiss and part. The rest is a reversion to the querying narrator of the opening and to Kathie's admission that she was more thrilled by his admiring her legs and fancying her than she would have been by talking about the topics she has wanted to hear him discuss since she was sixteen. "It's an awful thing to say, but that's how some women are. Even nice, sensible, fulfilled, happy women like Kathie Jones" (94). Drabble probably thinks worse of an earlier statement that, though Dan travels a lot, Kathie is "always so busy that she didn't miss him much" (52).

Not only women but "People like admiration more than anything" (94); the story equalizes humanity. Nobody would question telling a successful man he is handsome; successful women should not mind hearing about their good legs. We all should compliment and receive compliments. We are also all human in Wordsworthian terms and must therefore measure and regret our falling away from childhood aspirations and the impact they once had. Five years earlier, women could not accept their own common humanity.

Jenny in "A Day in the Life of a Smiling Woman."   In 1973, Drabble published another ironic female success story, "A Day in the Life of a Smiling Woman."[5] Jenny Jamieson seems from Rosamund's privileged set. Now in her thirties, she is a television personality. The narrator intrudes here as in "A Success Story," and much the same ambiguity results: "Probably you begin to see by now how sensible she was" (153). She is another sensitive, bright, lucky, talented, hardworking, modest Drabble female overcommitted to the word *lucky*.

Jenny learns the lesson the woman in the children's ward taught Rosamund Stacey: she can stop existing only for others and exist also for herself and need not always be polite and apologize. While her husband saw her becoming bored and used his influence to get her a "nice little job" at a television station, he could not know she would be a golden girl like upcoming Frances Wingate, would transfer her domestic efficiency to the work world, would offend no one and yet produce a good show, and would be admired and not disliked. What triggers the change in Jenny is the failure of her husband and her body or her failure of them. On the eve of the day we move through with her, she bares the rage she has suppressed against her now jealous, violent mate. The release is like an electric shock, and she knows that her smiling "mechanism" is broken forever.

The morning seems all right as she does her usual home chores, including shopping because she cannot depend on the baby-sitter, and then takes the bus into London because she is frightened of the traffic, not because she is so "sensible." The change breaks out at a committee meeting when she realizes her dislike for the members. At lunch with a clergyman who will be on her show, she is unable to "glow." She understands suddenly that she is treating adults like children when she drinks tonic, which looks like gin, so they will not be put off drinking. At the gynecologist's, her fear of dying of cancer prevents her hearing the answers to her "sensible" questions. Her thoughts are of her denial of her *woman's* body and of her children, her "grand passion" (152). She worries about breaking her contract with them for the period of their infancy. Her death will "disprove the existence of God" and ruin their "confidence in fate" (157).

Jenny's next "public" performance is guest of honor at a School Speech Day. As she sits on stage hoping her bleeding will not show, she has a soothing, though banal, epiphany. The "wings" of her spirit reveal that her "love is stronger than the grave" (163). She has gotten through life by clichés, quotations, touchstones, and old truths. Here are Karl (and Groucho) Marx, Freud, "luck run out," chance, "the apathy of God, the random blows of fate and the force for good and ill of human love" (157). She relies now on an emblematic scene like that at the end of *The Millstone*. At the school she sees baby fish in an inner glass tank to keep their mothers from eating them. With images that anticipate *The Realms of Gold* and

The Ice Age, Jenny wins beauty from decay: "Her solicitude [for her children's fish] had been more than godly, for God left dead dogs on beaches and crushed rabbits on the brows of roads. Gold spectacles, gold fillings, mounds of pilfering and salvage. But flesh is not for salvage: it is not even flotsam or jetsam. It is waste" (162).

Jenny does not die or maintain that pitch. She tells the school girls that they are "fortunate" in their "new opportunities" and that careers and husbands can be "easily combined" (164). The lie is no worse than her exorbitant mother love, her overprotectiveness, and her "contracts" with her children and God. Like the fish, they need an "inner glass tank" to protect them from their mother, who kills them again in the glibness she dispenses to their sisters in the school audience. Jenny's independence is only skin-deep.

Chapter Four
Helpless Women
The Waterfall

Drabble's fifth novel, *The Waterfall* (1969), is "wicked" because its "sublime, romantic passion" is not universal and its "idea that one can be saved from fairly pathological conditions by loving a man" (Hardin, 292–93) is dangerous. While it is controversial and evokes admiration and contempt, most find it a woman's story: Jane Gray, a poet, is sexually awakened and "saved" at age twenty-eight by an affair with James Otford, her cousin Lucy's husband.

Jane's husband, Malcolm, has left her, and she waits alone in her run-down Victorian house for the birth of her second child. Her son, Laurie, is with her parents, to whom she lies about Malcolm's absence. She at last calls Lucy and a midwife, and the child Bianca is named for the snow that falls just after her birth. James stays at night so Lucy can go home to their children and soon asks to be taken into Jane's bed. She is "drowning" in love for him before the doctor frees her for sexual consummation. Always maladroit with Malcolm, Jane, under James's tutelage, climaxes—"goes over the waterfall" of the title.

James establishes a virtual second home with Jane, and she feels she will die when he takes his real family to Italy on holiday. Her reclusiveness is broken only by their outings. In another Drabblean search for the past, they plan a trip to Norway, his ancestral home. On the way, James, against his wont, drives carefully; the ensuing accident is not his fault. Jane and the children are all right, but he goes into a coma. She has the presence of mind to pass herself off as his wife, but Lucy finds them.

When James recovers, they resume the affair although he is annoyed by the changes in Jane: no longer hopeless and helpless, she has returned to writing poetry and has employed help with the children and cleaned up the house. Malcolm does nothing more about his divorce suit, and the lovers exist as they were before the accident. Their one memorable weekend in Yorkshire seeing the

waterfall of Goredale Scar, another reference to the title, ends not
sublimely but ludicrously as James accidentally drinks talcum powder in his Scotch. The book ends with Jane's having developed
thrombosis and tentatively asserting her preference for suffering to
taking birth control pills with immunity.

Quintessential Drabble and more.   Jane is like and not like
the typical Drabble heroine. Sensitive, intelligent, and atypically
artistic, she carries the art of self-analysis to the extreme. While
she has found a career that can be combined with a family, she
seems not to notice or care and to have little sense of a vocation.
She was accepted at Oxford but not Cambridge and was disappointed
with her mediocre degree. Afterward, she took a London flat with
three other girls, found another "undistinguished" temporary job,
and drifted into marriage, at age twenty, after knowing Malcolm
for two years. She always meant to find another job after the wedding
but never did.

Customarily, the patterns Jane imposes catch her up. Willful
isolation from her parents and sister and a tendency to "split herself"
and go "underground" (120) become exaggerated in the marriage
until she simply sits and stares at the wall, passively waiting like
the stereotypical sacrificial victim while claiming to have nothing
in common with and no understanding of other women. Part of her
pathology derives from hatred of her parents and their Church of
England beliefs and "faintly clerical background" (52) and from the
family history of madness and suicide. Her "blood is blood" (49)
echoes *Jerusalem the Golden;* the family taint anticipates *The Realms
of Gold.* Her parents' foibles neatly reverse the Staceys'. While Jane
reacts against her background by passively resisting, the result is
the same: rigidification and the reduction of choices. As with Rosamund, these bear fruit in her men. Malcolm mounts a parallel
denial of his family, which is redeemed only in his mother's "bird-
like frail defiance" (100) and in his successful career as a classical
guitarist and singer. They are "exiles" from their roots, but Jane
finds Malcolm's rise misguided and "seeks out" her parents-in-law
"through social masochism, knowing that only by sinking could I
avoid the deadly, human, incriminating impulse to rise" (98).

Though Jane would "tell all," she is less forthcoming about her
reasons for taking up with James. A major source of his attraction,
as in *The Garrick Year,* is the outré. Scandal and rumors of financial
difficulties follow the Otfords and James. A poor driver of exciting

cars, he is entirely free of Malcolm's ambition. In escaping her family and Malcolm, Jane thus merely runs to the other end of the continuum and another extreme.

The unconventional also draws Jane to Lucy, who, with James, is her alter ego. The cousins were separated when Lucy went to America during the war. She reappears with a pronounced sense that Jane ought not just collect marbles but do something with them. Her assertiveness contrasts with Jane's diffidence and uneasiness about surface matters. Smart but lazy, Lucy *Gold*smith is another golden London bird cage type while Jane is a timid bird who would like to find a "familiar cage" (109). Lucy exits Cambridge with a bad degree and a reputation for sleeping around. She is the "pale queen" of Newnham (Drabble's college), who weeps as she de-wings countless male drones (127) and says that Jane is the only one who really knows her. She works quite successfully for a publishing firm, and she and James's mother have an affair with the same man. She manages easily her children and a career that is both practical and literary.

Lucy and Jane are a variation on Clelia-Clara and Louise-Sarah, and Drabble drew them in part from a close friend and herself (Poland, 263). Jane and her sister do not get along, but she admires Catherine's method of coping with their parents, quarreling openly but maintaining contact. Lucy, on the other hand, is Jane's "sister," "fate," and "example" (120) as Drabble's recurrent Freudianism pushes toward convergence of identity. They look alike, have "tremulous" outlines, and pass for each other in the course of the book. Their relationship remains ambivalent. Allies against their mothers, who timed their births within two weeks of each other, they are awkward together because their parents assume that they will be close.

The sexual control of Lucy's mother issues in her daughter's promiscuity, but Lucy evinces no guilt. Jane's rebellion becomes ineptitude in adolescence, when she faints at the instructions on a Tampax box; frigidity in the marriage bed; and general helplessness before all practical matters. Her guilt is both general, from her religious background, and specific, from her failures at all the tasks other women perform naturally. She is an expanded portrait of Phillipa Denham, missing her fate by getting the right man. Even with James, however, she is so sensitive she can hear cloth shriek before the needle and so impractical she cannot place bread in a breadbox or a lid on anything.

Jane is equally unfit for motherhood. She is "scared out of her wits" (105) when she gets pregnant and relieved when she miscarries. She experiences "the same cycle of resentment and nonacceptance" (108) with Laurie, the separation between body and mind that has plagued her since childhood. The birth is easy and thoroughly Drabblean: "The first baby's a kind of trick, the way one feels so well afterward" (24). She nonetheless lives divided between "the anxious intelligent woman and the healthy and efficient mother" (108), a split that is counterpointed by the two Janes telling the story, the alternating first- and third-person narrators.[1] Laurie is marked by her strangeness.

Lucy, in contrast, lived with James and married him only when she had to. Their ease at domesticity and his success with the children amaze Jane and send her searching wildly for their "secret of matrimony, the secret key to being a woman, and living with a man" (135). The children prevent Jane's "dottiness" (Hardin, 290) from spilling over into complete madness and preserve her until James, who would not have found her but for Bianca. Even before Malcolm left, she forced herself to take tea with other mothers so Laurie would have playmates, and her observations at the nursery school induce enough distancing to recognize additional kinds of craziness (241–42). When James is in Italy, the children's welfare combats her lethargy and makes her take them to the zoo. They counter her fixation that, if she were drowning, she could not reach out a hand to save herself because she would not oppose her fate in loving James (7). He may be her "fate," "luck," "grace," and other Drabble paraphernalia, but her first thought in the wreck is the children, and she "would have wished him dead, poor love, to spare them" (221). They, like Octavia Stacey, let in reality and turn her from helplessness, not allowing her to take "refuge in sensibility or hysteria" (204).

Integration and interconnectedness.   The healthy person has body and soul in balance; Jane has always shortchanged the first. Drabble doses her with an excess of "being in the body"[2] until she surfeits and moves toward balance. Many clues cite the need for integration and fight the extremes of the continua she imposes on experience. Her denial of family leads to overimmersion in the "Freudian family nexus" (137) with Lucy and James. Her mother's sexual control is answered first with frigidity and then with an over-indulgence (James) as extreme as Lucy's. The repulsiveness of the wetness of the marriage bed becomes acceptance of Malcolm's accusation of lesbianism to have an excuse for avoiding sex altogether, the embarrassing blood and sweat of the bed in which she gives birth to Bianca and attracts James, the waterfall with him, and, last, petulance when he fails to take her over it. The "close heat" of the room that protects newborn Bianca and will "surely generate its own salvation" (10) becomes the passion between Jane and James.

The commingling does not go unnoticed by Jane, though she continues to reduce it to one of its strands, salvation through James. She links pregnancy and old age (22) and so emphasizes her own assumed, unnecessary helplessness. She cries "like a child" when she wants to write poetry and cannot and wants to have James and cannot. She sees the world conspire not to let her know the horrors of marriage and childbirth (103) and the sameness of sexual love and maternity (140, 173). Parents tell their children to play together and just as thoughtlessly, to marry and love together (123–25). Playing nursery games and choosing teams portend the "savage" game of sexual selection (130–31), but Jane ignores the positive side—the children's fairy tale that lets blue roses (possibility) live and is, simultaneously, about the hardships of "grown-up" love. When Jane experiences sexual climax, with James, for the first time, she images its effects as their mutual rebirth, with each becoming the offspring of the other (159). The resonance is still of obsession, to the point that the images of maternity are pillaged to service desire. Jane, a poet, ought to know more of the difference between simile and metaphor than Jenny Jamieson, who also confuses maternal and sexual love.

The penultimate nexus confirms Jane's analogies and tentative linkages, though without her complete comprehension. James's card trick, one of the "waterfalls" of the title, though Drabble denies originally being aware of its doubleness (Hardin, 291), is performed to distract Laurie and is fused with sexual experience in marriage. The cards were a wedding gift to Jane and Malcolm, who played poker. When James talks about those who do such tricks "badly through not caring" (155), Drabble is commenting on the Grays' mutual culpability in their failed marriage. Another element latent in the scene is luck. The card trick "doesn't always work"; neither children nor adults can expect to be perpetually entertained; true lovers do not always or even frequently find each other. The episode lets in reality without destroying possibility.

The scene with the waterfall of cards also forecasts the ultimate nexus, Goredale Scar. Jane draws analogies between James's prowess with the cards and her craft as a poet. He has learned his art from a "literary" source, the American western, and she sees it as inexplicably significant like the form and symmetry of verse. The natural waterfall is an example of the true sublime and is, like poetry, "impressive not through size . . . but through form." It balances "wildness" and "bodily limit" (253) as Jane must balance her tendency toward aberration in psyche and love to accommodate children and others and yet free her distinctive and individual talents as a poet and a person. Significant, too, is the fact that they make the trip at Jane's insistence and despite James's bad leg.[3] She is beginning to exist between solipsism and self-abnegation.

Literature in *The Waterfall*.   Jane denies her strength of will and is victimized by the persona she adopts. She forgets that her passivity and helplessness are self-chosen, manufactured. To break from them, she imposes "classic" literary situations, thus, like Rosamund Stacey, using literature reductively. She has had ample opportunity to realize her mistakes prior to James. Her family is of the "genteel middle-class descent" described by Jane Austen, so, loathing it, she loathes that author (56, 59–60, 98). She is not interested in Malcolm until he sings a Thomas Campion lyric about death, which she finds as blameworthy as Shakespeare's love at first sight and Romeo's demand to have Juliet "because she is the one that will kill me" (92) and which confirms her desire to be a "doomed romantic" (91). They meet when Malcolm performs at a party given by the teacher of her Elizabethan literature class, and her admission that she does not like music[4] would have cued the Elizabethans to her flaws. Despite her appropriating *Romeo and Juliet,* however, she is shocked that her marriage ends with Malcolm's violently beating her head against the bedroom wall and paraphrases its "These violent delights have violent ends" (187) on the eve of the Norway trip. She recognizes the fatality of her married name, "Jane Gray," a memory of the historical (and literary) woman who went "on the block" for love, yet makes a pun at her daughter's expense when she names Bianca (42).

The affair is recast along literary lines throughout and is excused as an example of Seneca's "in jumping to avoid our fate, we meet

it" (102, 243–44). Jane's imagery of drowning is justified by the
Emily Dickinson poem serving as epigraph. While Jane waits to
recover from childbirth, she adds literary foreshadowing by fearing
that James will die in a car accident before she can go to bed with
him and likens their enforced separation to "Tristram's sword" (40).[5]
Later she becomes Tennyson's "Mariana at the moated grange" (141)
waiting for James's visits. Theirs is one of "those tales of entranced
lovers kept alive through the years by faith, those fables of sleepers
and dreamers awoken finally by the intensity and endurance of
desire" (230). Drabblean Jane is fascinated by men in fast cars, and
she makes that fascination and James, who is her intellectual inferior,
palatable by linking them with early death and Keats (87), whose
short life has always been her gauge for achievement (83).

To excuse and ennoble, Jane looks for signs that they, like great
literary couples, were "fated" to love, and she weaves their story in
literary fashion with image chains and symbolism. There are the
leitmotiv of drowning in passion, original at least in the use of the
waterfall; the alternate burning of passion and freezing from fear of
its loss, borrowed from the Elizabethans; the stones (68–69, 87,
97, 174, 195, 216) that link Jane and James and suggest her
hardening of her heart toward Malcolm; the albatross (89, 134,
241), the classic guilt symbol from Coleridge's "The Rime of the
Ancient Mariner"; and the plant images that figure forth her survival
(42, 193) and James's (211, the mutant holly tree).

Jane's choice of André Gide's *La Porte étroite* and James's of Emile
Zola's *Thérèse Raquin* become examples of the felicitous conjunction
of true lovers, no matter that they are "short sad read[s]" whose
contents should warn or that the lies she and Malcolm tell their
parents are, by the same line of reasoning, just as true signs of
oneness. Jane sees herself as Thomas Hardy's Sue Bridehead in *Jude
the Obscure* and George Eliot's Maggie Tulliver in *The Mill on the
Floss;* the injured James becomes the earl of Gloucester in Shakespeare's *King Lear* and Rochester in Charlotte Brontë's *Jane Eyre.*
Jane confuses herself not only with literary characters and, in real
life, with Lucy, but with the authors of such characters—with
Charlotte Brontë (89) or John Galsworthy (251–52) or Emile Zola
(138), for example. She seems to be looking for a way to live her
life in someone else, including James, or in some fixed role (Emily
Dickinson/poet, mother, mistress, romantic heroine) rather than

building an independent life. Her true helplessness resides in this failure rather than in its surface manifestations of impracticality.

Jane's admissions that James changed her forever and that she is "now what he made" (246) do not take us far, for she is still seeing him as an end in himself. More acceptable is her sense that she is "no longer capable of inaction" (54), but the true change is measured as much by her use of literature as by the changes in her domestic habits and by her critical glances at James's laborious detailing of the accident. The albatross, once the symbol only of her guilt and egocentricity, turns outward; she cannot purge Malcolm of his sense of guilty responsibility for her until she regularizes her life and household. Her neglected house plant, one of Drabble's favorite symbols in the book (Hardin, 64), must survive aridity and freezing as Jane leaves spiritual sterility and frozen human communication for the wetness and heat of her passion for James and survives those too. Her basket contains "watery tender streaks of green" (222) portending not only James's recovery but her own. She connects them with Keats and so refines her earlier application of him to the premature deaths of men in cars.

Jane goes on to connect that green color with poetry, to choose it over James, and to settle her vocation in familiar terms: "I would write, because writing is the thing that one can do anywhere, in a hotel bedroom, in solitary confinement [another sign of recovery since she has previously named this her worst fear], in a prison cell, a defense more final, less destructible, than the company of love. I could feel it stirring in me. Descending. I could see the changes in the color of the air,[6] the faintly approaching presences of words" (233). Her metaphors of descent into passion are reclaimed and redeemed by the descent of inspiration. Once Jane wrote to console herself with the imposition of form on despair. She stereotyped the literary impulse after Shelley's "falling on the thorns of life and bleeding": the unhappier she was, the more she wrote. Now she is her own writer able to create from and respond to "the experience without the loss: for free" (250) and no longer having to cast herself as a Victorian trying to be a romantic.

Jane survives the fact that her great love is not of the epic cast. "All true fictional lovers die" (207), but real people are seldom allowed such heightening, such "feminine" endings. She has to be weighed in the balance with Lucy, the wife. In one of the "old novels," she would pay the price of death (256) for her betrayal of her cousin. As it stands, she is a "modern woman" paying in both thrombosis and neurosis, in comedy rather than tragedy (250), in an ordinary white rose (217) rather than a blue one, and in James's blood-spattered real shirt rather than the "bloody cloth" of the fairy tale (210). In the light of renewed sense, the Herculean labors she has manufactured for James pale beside Malcolm's "continuing to pay with no returns" (217). The lush, Freudian complexity of fused identities yields to an analogy with "some dreadful Elizabethan comedy of impersonation and substitution and mistaken identity" (223). She can survive, too, the plunge from the sublime (Goredale Scar) to the ridiculous (Scotch and talcum powder), the last great continuum whose extremes all humans are capable of in limited quantities. As she and James look upon the sublime, she is able to identify a bird flying there as a curlew. She makes that identification from poetry, a healthy use of literature and another sign of her recovery.

Drabble explodes several stereotypes in Jane, among them the passive female, feminine ineptitude, and immersion of the self in the classic love affair. The great achievement of the novel is that, for all Jane's initial repulsiveness, the reader can finally appreciate her and the process of her growth.

The Helpless and Hopeless

"The Reunion." Jane voyages to Cythera, the isle of Venus, and returns, for, although she still has James, she is less dependent on him already and senses that she will be claimed by Malcolm.[7] In two short stories published just prior to *The Waterfall*, the return remains doubtful.

In "The Reunion" (1968), the former lovers accidentally meet at their old rendezvous. Brought to the area by practicalities, they feel compelled to the café by the habits and "ghosts" of their year together. Like Jane and James, they are victims of their own romanticism, which has made them give each other up for the sake of renunciation, though they pretend to part for their spouses and children. They now delight in detailing the ritual of parting and the changes in intensity of hurt over time. They are fate-ridden, acknowledge "nature, damnation and destiny"[8] in their reunion, and could play the lovers Paolo and Francesca in Dante's *Inferno*. During the affair, they spent most of their time talking of its "impossibility," and both were "insatiable, merciless deliverers of ultimatums," of "preparation for death" (154) by separation.

Encountering even one ingredient of the atmosphere in which James entered her bed makes Jane grow faint (32). These other "disastrous romantics" "habitually connived with fate by remembering the names of restaurants and the streets they had once walked along as lovers." Kenneth tells Viola that "those who do not forget will meet again" (168). Like James, he is as involved in the romantic trappings of the relationship as the woman, and he describes their "Proustian experience." Yet Viola applies the imagery of falling, feels faint and trembles, and tried to assign the effects to "proximity." She would have gone on forever giving ultimatums and retreating from them. Kenneth at length tired of the game and ceased to call. While his love has renewed in her presence, she has "very nearly" slept with no one in the three years since their parting. Having *fallen* not only into love but into the literary pattern of love, she is more helpless than Jane the poet, whose appreciation of form and distancing brings extrication.

"A Voyage to Cythera." "A Voyage to Cythera" (1967) also suggests that women feel more intensely. Fated like Jane by her name, Helen is, ironically, a spinster. She is another romantic but with an additional obsession. She loves the "delighted terror"[9] produced by trains and is fascinated with all "emblems of departure" (98). Her erotic dreams are of destinations, not men, and she disavows a friend's linking of "new places" with the possibility of falling in love. A Budapest train makes "her skin tighten and her hair stand on end" (98), reactions akin to Jane's hearing Malcolm sing the Campion lyric and Viola's meeting Kenneth again.

Despite her reliance on literal transport for her "deliberately romantic embarkations" (99), Helen is an "expert" on love as obsession and disease and knows instantly the malady of the man who enters her train compartment: he is "still rapt in the first five minutes of love, that brief and indefinite breathless pause before familiarity, affection, disillusion, rot, decay" (99). Cherishing the "moment of expectation before revelation" (98), he yet hopes that actuality will match imagination. The alternate burning and freezing demarking love since the Elizabethans ought to forewarn him, but he persists, his senses so heightened that he can recognize Helen's affinity. With the "peculiar mixture of diffidence and vanity" (99) that usually marks Drabble women, he asks Helen to address and post his letter to the woman causing his misery.

Helen yields but resents the incident "because it did so much to vindicate her own crazy expectancy, her foolish faith in revelation" while her "saner self" knows better. She seeks out the addresses and "some possible other country of the passions" (149), and fate brings her to an "island" where the curtains are open, the lights are on, and women and children eat and decorate for Christmas. She sees "things too vague to name, of happiness, of hope, of brightness, warmth, and celebration." The emotion in the room is "like water unimaginably profound" (150). With Wordsworth and Yeats, she has only the vision of intimacy.

As the curtains are drawn and Helen is left with her image in the window, the man from the train arrives and voices his fears for her fragility. Symbolically, she may break from "wasted opportunities," from being cut off from engagement with life. What she witnesses goes beyond the nexus of love, children, and literature in *The Waterfall* as the two women take "a kind of soft rapt delight" in each other (150) like Rose and Emily in *The Needle's Eye*. As in the Rainer Maria Rilke poem that prefaces the story, Helen's beloved is "lost to begin with," is "gardens" never entered. [10]

Daphne, Julian, and Stephen. Daphne in *A Summer Bird-Cage* is plain, frumpy, and not clever and causes more problems for Sarah than for herself. Her cousin mistakes her lack of luck for helplessness and hopelessness. At the Tate Gallery, she is not nearly so embarrassed as Sarah, has the tact to avoid family gossip, and is audacious enough to make a pass at Lovell. The thoughtful privileged patronize in applying the stereotype of quiet desperation to the Daphnes of the world.

Julian in *The Garrick Year* and Stephen in *The Realms of Gold* are as maladjusted as Phillipa Denham, and both end as suicides. The first is imprisoned by his appearance and his maleness: he will always look homosexual and too young to play major stage roles, and no mother with children could afford the luxury of drowning.

Stephen is less specifically helpless and hopeless. Drawn to and repelled by Frances's energy, he wonders how she can "possibly imagine" her actions "worth doing" (74). A certain fatality and cosmic grief hang about him as about Phillipa. Nothing accounts fully for his spiritual pathology—not the family depression; the Jewish destiny inherited from his mother; the obsessive fear of diseases his daughter may be prey to; doubts of Freud's claim that the self longs for life more than death; his wife Beata's belief that living is a crime; the concatenation of Beata, Sebastian, and Aunt Con; or brooding too long on Salvator Rosa's painting of Empedocles leaping into Etna unsubdued. The best we can believe is that Stephen too is unlucky. He lacks the "gift" of weeping (299) and going on of Frances and Karel. Phillipa could weep but not put aside weeping to go on. Drabble has drawn another human continuum with weeping, but then moving on, both the center and the way.

Chapter Five
The Helpless Independent

The Needle's Eye

Longer and more substantial, *The Needle's Eye* (1972) is a thesis novel that approaches the worldview of *The Ice Age* and employs male and female protagonists, Simon Camish and Rose Vertue Vassiliou. Fitful feminism[1] remains, but Drabble is concerned about human issues generally. When the *Guardian* asked for an article on child custody, she wrote the book instead,[2] and children cause a new kind of entrapment in this sixth book. Rose returns to Christopher because, morally, she cannot deprive him of his offspring or them of their father, a decision that costs her potential happiness with Simon and, ironically, erodes her spiritual progress. The book is about surviving the human situation, choosing among flawed alternatives, and being privileged. Though Rose is not beautiful, very young (in her early thirties), highly intelligent, or well educated, she is rich. Her nanny has reinforced Matthew 19.23–24, and Rose must know if a camel can go through the eye of a needle more easily than the rich can enter heaven. She is convinced of the necessity for effort and struggle cited in the epigraph from William Butler Yeats on the "fascination of what's difficult." Drabble may also remember his "Too much sacrifice can make a stone of the heart."[3]

The Needle's Eye opens with Simon observing a communal world, the off-license, from which he is self-exiled. He stops in on his way to a dinner party to purchase a gift for his hosts. It, too, is flawed, but he does meet Rose there, and she, drawn by his being a lawyer, tells him her story and begins to engage him in another and greater communal effort. She is the heiress whose father made her a ward of the court to stop her marrying a poor Greek boy and who renewed her notoriety by giving away thirty thousand pounds to build an African school.

The Vassiliou marriage is seriocomic in the telling, though it involves attempted suicide, rape, and mutual abuse whose extreme comes with Rose throwing a child downstairs in a fit of anger. Their passion was spent prior to marrying, and at best the question was Wordsworthian: what to make of a diminished thing. Domestic horror, however, is not what Rose would jettison with Christopher. Her quest is positive: to live an independent life on her own terms, hurting as few people as possible. Her route (abnegation) may be simple, but the impossibility of living without one's choices affecting others brings complication.

When Simon meets Rose, her independence is threatened; Christopher is bringing a custody suit, founded on her dottiness and denial of a proper education for the children, which is likely to go against her. She is contemplating yielding when Christopher pretends to kidnap the children and carry them abroad. She learns from her son that they are actually going to Bryanston Hall, her parents' East Anglia estate, and Simon drives her there. On the way, they admit their love and accept the responsibilities preventing their marrying. The novel could have ended with the visit to the sea shared by Christopher, Rose, Simon, and the Vassiliou children, but Simon participates grudgingly, family bickering erupts, and Rose's recollection of a corpse complements the literal and figurative evocations of death on the journey from London to Bryanston Hall. The scene is reminiscent of the snake in the sheep's belly at the end of *The Garrick Year*.

Worse, this novel bares the future. Simon remains an observer. Rose returns to Christopher, and Simon watches her gradually lose the grace she has won. A kind of community is gained nonetheless as Simon goes about with Rose, her friend Emily, and all of their children. His wife, Julie, has been born again in his mind through her friendship with Rose. The world that emerges takes its tone of diminished acceptance from Wordsworth's later poems. Its emblem is the toothless lion fronting the Alexandra Palace where the group goes to see a mundane dog show. Unlike the aristocratic beasts at Bryanston Hall, it is "a beast of the people. Mass-produced it had been, but it had weathered into identity," Rose's hope "for every human soul" (382).

John Bunyan and *The Needle's Eye*. The earlier novels occasionally give the impression that their literary allusions are gratuitous. In *The Needle's Eye*, for the first time, the protagonists are not connected with the literary world. Yet literature informs this book and merges virtually perfectly with it. As if to provide an alternative to *The Millstone*, in which scholarly Rosamund "misuses" literature and links herself with John Bunyan, Drabble makes his *Grace Abounding* and *The Pilgrim's Progress* the principal backdrop.

The needle text "Puritan" Noreen imposes on Rose is comparable to Bunyan's experiences with a passage in Ecclesiasticus, with Martin Luther's *Commentary on Galatians,* and with his fear of "selling Christ," detailed in his spiritual autobiography, *Grace Abounding. The Needle's Eye* is spiritual *biography*—of Rose and Simon in particular but also of Everyperson. Its division into two parts corresponds to the pilgrimages of Christian and Christiana in *The Pilgrim's Progress.* The suggestive, symbolic names of Drabble's characters evoke the allegorical and spiritual abstractions of Bunyan. Rose's middle name of *Vertue* is the most obvious, but her first is reminiscent of the "multifoliate rose" (Mary) of Catholic tradition and of the "rose of England." Simon triggers overtones of Simon Peter, especially when he employs an image-chain of stones/rocks. They echo not only "upon this rock I will build my church" (Matthew 16.18) but the hardness of heart against which Simon struggles and which Rose's family, the Bryan*ston(e)s,* exemplifies. Both Rose and Simon climb Bunyan's Hill Difficulty. "Camish" contrasts with "Cane-ish" and reminds us through its evocation of the River Cam that this story, like Bunyan's, is also about a nation.

Rose seeks grace for herself and brings it to others. She causes water to spring from the dry rock that is the besetting sin of Simon and Julie and so baptizes the wife in the husband's eyes, as is forecast by the moment when she assumes Julie's identity (309). Christopher, whose name is leavened with Christ and Lucifer, is also a transmuter. He can transform the aridity of the real world into a "moonlit jungle" (323). A mixture of good and bad, he holds his own children for the ransom of Rose's spirit, thus recalling his wife to the sense of family and communal duty so strong in Bunyan. Ironically, he also counterpoints the ransom of Christ, while Rose, the true Christ-figure, "bleeds in her mind" (273), cuts her thumb with a razor, and bears as her "seal" (of the redeemed in Revelation and Bunyan) the scar where she has attempted to cut her wrist. Like Christ, she is drawn to the outcast, dispossessed (Christopher [87]), and maimed (her childhood friend Joyce) of the world.

The use of precedents further reminds us of the general application of the book. Prior to her divorce case, Rose visits the court to observe another. Christopher perhaps gets the idea for his mock-kidnapping from the newspaper accounts of Mr. Calvacoressi, who flees with his children to Italy and whose name contains possible plays on "Calvary" and *cor,* "heart" (and is also the name of an Italian friend of Arnold Bennett mentioned several times in Drabble's biography of that author).

Rose and Simon stand poised on the brink of Bunyan's "wilderness of this world," and his "strait and narrow" way recalls the strain associated with the "needle's eye" and the emphasis on difficulty that pervades Drabble's book from the epigraph. Rose's family, like Christian's, thinks her crazy, as does the whole world. The Hill Lucre, the silver mine of Demas, and Sloth are of as little importance to Rose as to Bunyan, but his village of Morality and such characters as Mr. Legality and Formalist are rewritten in Drabble's Dickensian assault on the British legal system. The law flounders before the moral complexities: the relation of the trees and the wood (205); the defense of the wrong case for the right reason (251); the individual's spiritual integrity vis-à-vis the good of one's husband and children; the virtue of knowing right if one does not practice it; grace that cannot be earned but still must be sought; the spirit that "bloweth whither it listeth" (149); the spirit that kills while the letter gives life (257); the question of whether a "good" education can be provided by the neighborhood state school; the inability of right to exalt itself as *Peter* Harold *Stone,* a good man and good headmaster, provides a sterile affidavit on the education of Rose's children and as Mrs. Flanagan attempts to testify for Rose and loses her voice; Rose's sacrifice of chastity to hospitality when she goes to bed with Anton rather than apprise him of their linguistic impasse. The list could go on; Bunyan's and Drabble's landscapes partake of the dilemmas of Abraham sacrificing Isaac and of Solomon trying to find the true mother or Bertolt Brecht's treatment in *The Caucasian Chalk Circle* (272, 274). Drabble updates Bunyan's contrast of "carnal/moral" conversion, the pharisaical fulfillment of the letter, rather than of the spirit, of the biblical Law, with true faith.

At the end, Rose tells Christopher and Simon about a dead body she once thought she saw near the sea, her version of Christian's "burden." She has carried the image on her bony shoulders like a dead bird (271) and in her bloody, bat soul (379). It reappears in the dead creatures lining the roads of England. She loses this burden when she and Simon stand before the carcass of the dangling stoat (307) to declare their mutual passion and relinquish it simultaneously. Leaving that place, she makes her peace with her past and moves to the penultimate moment by the sea when she can talk about the dead person. Not Christ, she cannot literally renew life in the waters, but she acclimates. Forgiveness has pulsed through her from the moment she met Christopher in the garden, another association with Christ. Her spirit has moved to acceptance (316). She will fall away again—she does so before the seaside picnic is at an end—but she will be renewed. Drabble refuses to accept that conclusion as defeatist.[4]

Simon lives perpetually in Bunyan's Slough of Despond. He combines the Giant Despair and his wife Diffidence, the inhabitants of Doubting Castle. His dryness (18, 19) is Bunyan's spiritual aridity. He is both very like Rose and very different from her. They share Bunyan's "spiritual thinness," but Simon's derives from a negative withdrawal and withholding of the self; Rose's, from continuous struggle to do right in defiance of imperfection. Negative about the world and himself, Simon endures quietly. Wrong with his mother, his wife, and his children, he is most wrong in his disengagement; in refusing to engage with them, he refuses to wrestle with the angel of despair or with Bunyan's Apollyon for his own soul.

Simon has no exact counterpart in Bunyan. Unlike Ignorance, who lacks a "certificate" of entrance to the Celestial City, he knows what is right but is self-paralyzed. He will never be, like Bunyan's Christian and like Rose, "sick of desire for the Master." He wants grace, and his spirit, with its Rose-like "feathered bony shoulders," struggles in the "net" (134), an image strong in Bunyan and Rose; but we find his narration lacking in cogency. He is a masterful characterization of the "cold fish," saved from the stereotype because he would not be cold. Drabble says that we underrate his positive actions because he underrates them.[5] She rewards him with fitful hierophanies and apocalyptic visions. The luckiest Drabble person is the one, like Rose, who knows right and acts on it. But Simon and Clara (*Jerusalem the Golden*) have the vision but will never be lost in the overflow of powerful feeling. They will always be outsiders watching the Celestial City from the wrong side of the river. Simon's use of Bunyanesque diction to contrast the "stinking dirty clarty water" and the "golden river" (129) expresses his perpetual submission to letter rather than spirit. Yet he wants to want the spirit and does not, for example, cease until he finds that Violet Bank was once a violet bank (130). His sterile vision of the "day when the world shall turn to grass once more, and the tender flowers will break and buckle the great paving stones" (131), unlike Clara's, finds paradise unpeopled.

Neither is Simon able to give himself by letting others give to him. He uses the great Christ image of the pelican feeding its young with its blood (30) for his mother's sacrifices for him but remains guilt-ridden toward her despite her refusal to accept the doctrine of the inevitability of "the course of destruction." Her son accepts its wickedness but believes the doctrine true. He knows that he cannot be happy if he destroys others' lives, but he cannot understand that not participating in those lives is a kind of destruction. On the one occasion when he does act and participate—by telling Christopher to stop being divisive and live with Rose—the gesture is meaningless on his own account because he feels it "beautifully to his own disadvantage" and takes "some satisfaction from the thought that any gain would be his own loss" (281–82).

Rose, in contrast, is flesh and blood. Hers is a wayfaring/warfaring struggle in the Bunyanesque, Pauline tradition. She is etiolated physically, not spiritually. Peopled only by the gentlemanly spiritual like Simon, the world might just wind down; its vital animal spirit already lies bleeding along the roadsides and byways of England. Born in a silken cocoon, her origins the opposite of Bunyan's and Simon's, Rose expresses the great belief of *The Pilgrim's Progress* in the myriad ways of reaching heaven, though Bunyan would never have thought to place a rich person on the road to salvation.

In *Grace Abounding,* God is "after" the child Bunyan with dreams and visions to lure him from sin. Rose has these, Noreen, and Bunyan himself (342–47). She, too, has been "fated" to be what she is and to make a journey as "extraordinary" (310–11) as his. She is a "divided self" (274–75), the label William James used for Bunyan.[6] Drabble's title aligns itself with Bunyan's difficulties in squeezing through the gap in the wall in the vision of the Bedford women in *Grace Abounding,* and the conundrum that it posits gets at the hostility Rose feels (and Bunyan felt before her) between her actual and ideal selves and the relation between faith and works. She and Christopher have lived together (89) in Bunyan's "mire" or "quag," and she questions why she is not allowed to pursue quietly in (symbolic) Middle Road the life that she chooses (157, 275).

Like Bunyan's, Rose's spiritual journey alternates lapses and gains, battles and mind work. In *The Pilgrim's Progress,* the lions that block

Christian's way to the Palace Beautiful are actually chained, as he learns from the Porter Watchful; in *The Needle's Eye,* Rose comes to accept the difference between the false lions of Bryanston Hall and the "weathered lion" of the Alexandra Palace, home of the dog show. In part 2 of *The Pilgrim's Progress,* the pilgrims knock at the Wicket-gate but are frightened by a dog, whose danger is another self-delusion. In the Interpreter's House, Bunyan's second group of pilgrims is treated to a series of emblems in the Significant Rooms, including a hen and chicks and a garden with a variety of flowers. Rose discovers the chickens and the armchair on the bombed site (227). While she cannot explicate their meaning, she knows their meaningfulness. In turn, she becomes the Interpreter showing the emblematic scene to Simon and so fulfills Bunyan's theme of each pilgrim as exemplar for the next.

Rose and Christopher, while still estranged from her family, make a surreptitious trip to Bryanston Woods and climb the wall as Milton's Satan scales the natural wall of Eden in *Paradise Lost,* another Puritan vision. They become Bunyan's By-ends, but the negative connotations of Bunyan and Milton are ultimately transcended when the barriers to Bryanston Hall, like its stone lions, are broken down. Rose enters in disguise when she returns there with Simon, but, when she exits, the only remaining holdout from the community of friends is her mother, who, like Bunyan's Ignorance, is thus denied access to the Celestial City as she stands on its very threshold.

Part 2 of *The Pilgrim's Progress* is traditionally read as a communal and "female" vision and as Bunyan's apologia to the women of his congregation. While part 2 of *The Needle's Eye* is longer than part 1 and is an account of how Rose finds community and sacrifices her individuality for others' needs, it continues to share its stage with Simon, whose acclimation to circumstance, if less spectacular than Rose's, is nonetheless real. In some sense, part 1 is Rose's version of *Grace Abounding*—an account of a life's effort to find grace. Bunyan receives the reward of the title but ends with an admission that he still suffers from seven temptations, among them his leaning to the works of the Law rather than to the spirit of Christ. If anything, Rose's crisis, presented as Christopher and the law renewing the whole struggle for the children and, indirectly, her hold on the life of grace, dominates Drabble's part 1. We learn about it before we get the account of her pilgrimage to independence. Moreover, where Christiana and the children are drawn to pilgrimage (part 2) by Christian's model (part 1), Simon, though already set in the right way, follows Rose's lead in both parts. She becomes his "case of conscience," a standard seventeenth-century genre used by Bunyan, as the Turkish Cypriot husband in the divorce court becomes Rose's, however much she would like to side with his English wife through loyalty to her own sex (90).

Part 2 of *The Needle's Eye* is another kind of pilgrimage in which Rose learns to subordinate her individual grace. In Drabble's words, "to stop short at self-realisation, and the achieving of one's own identity, is to refuse to move into the eighth stage [of Erik Erikson's ages of man], in which . . . one assumes responsibility for one's community and one's succeding [*sic*] generations."[7] While Drabble did not read Erikson until after she had written this book, these same responsibilities are met by Bunyan in part 2 of *The Pilgrim's Progress,* in which there is also talk of kidnapping—by the Giant Maul, a sophist, and, seasonally, by a monster who attacks the reformed Vanity Fair to steal children. Innkeeper Gaius warns Christiana to get her children married to insure that her husband's name will be carried on, and there are not only marriages but pregnancy, baby-sitting, and children crying out for help. Christian is dead, but his route and mementos and emblems of his struggle are available to his family. Christian, however, gave up nothing for that family. Indeed, he stuck his fingers in his ears and ran off crying after eternal life. Rose had no children when she first went on pilgrimage, but she had parents and money. Later, she flees husband and money but tries to cling to the children. When she sees the harm to them and their father, she returns, helpless, to her "non-self" (190).

Drabble's children, like Bunyan's, not only take but give. Rose's older son, Konstantin, with his oboe playing and his peripatetic teacher, links *The Needle's Eye* with the music of beatitude (also suggested in Emily's last name, "Offenbach") and the wandering motif in *The Pilgrim's Progress.* He exemplifies the "constancy" implicit in his name. One of the few children we come to know despite their omnipresence in Drabble's novels, he is loyal to both parents, and it is he who lets Rose know that Christopher has not truly kidnapped her children. Wise beyond his years, he also serves as a kind of moral monitor for his mother, whom he pulls up short with the observation that she is a "whited sepulchre" (172) when she talks about now being bored with children.

Simon's son, Dan, who possesses another biblical name, is in the negative exemplary mode of *The Pilgrim's Progress*. The "sins of his father" are visited on him, the product of a loveless marriage. A virtual illiterate and psychotic, he sits forlornly in the kitchen with a noncommunicative maid while his parents play at hospitality in the dining room. Again, Simon sees what is needed if he cannot act. At the end, however, Rose pulls Dan into her communal circle with the other children.

Children in *The Needle's Eye* are generally in that special category Drabble labels survivors. If Simon has Dan, he also has Kate, a "survivor" for whom he has "hopes" (193). Helen, though like her mother, nevertheless asks Simon if people "can help what they grow up like" (193). Exiled from Rose by the family trip to Cornwall at Easter (another of the novel's religiously charged temporal markings), Simon has his cross lightened by establishing contact with his children in Kate. Like Rose, he undergoes his own (demi-)journey to family duty and community.

Rose may have reached Bunyan's Beulah after all, for it is a place where there is no distinction between the sexes. Emily, Simon, Rose, occasionally Christopher and Julie, and all the children share small moments; but these are "like a new contract [again the merging of biblical and legal], like the rainbow after the flood" (227). They are the "little movements of the spirit in its daily routine" that Drabble describes Arnold Bennett writing about.[8] They turn Simon's "ghostly white crumpled bud of a rose" (76) into Rose. They are the pure moment Simon's mother experiences in an Oxford garden. They grow large when, on Whit Saturday, the National Gardens Scheme opens Bryanston Hall to the public, and Rose's forgiveness begins to ooze forth in the green that stripes Simon's mind (312). They change Bunyan's Vanity Fair into the communal ritual of buying that Simon witnesses at the opening. They are more than most of us get, but we might think them less than sexual passion. As is customary in Drabble, however, sex does not loom large. The attraction between Rose and Christopher spent itself before their marriage. Simon seems never to have known it, though he is, miraculously, not the bloodless creature such an observation might make him. Rose has reached a plane where sex seems not to matter much, and she draws Simon there (164).

Rationally, when we reach the day where there is "no marriage and no giving in marriage," relationships should be easier; the fact that we do not question such an outcome emotionally is a testimony to the deftness with which Drabble has set forth *The Needle's Eye.* She nonetheless never lets us forget that there is a caterpillar among Rose's pressed-flower collection. Konstantin points out that it can be found on page ten (229). One of the beauties of *The Needle's Eye* is that, so much in the mode of Bunyan's allegories, it is yet so unallegorical, as Bunyan's own works are.

Drabble's "Ms. Dead-ends" and "Ms. All-ends" complement Bunyan's By-ends. The first, Eileen, the working-class girl, has no possibilities. She becomes pregnant by a married garageman and deposits her child Sharon (another biblical echo—the "rose of Sharon") with her mother, Rose's neighbor. But Rose is wrong to write her epitaph (264). Eileen, in the mode of Bunyan's *The Life and Death of Mr. Badman,* falls in with a shady gang, gets shot in the leg, and is "deeply transfigured by pain and notoriety" (370). Nonetheless, she is very different from Ms. All-ends, "lovely Miss Lindley" (151–53), Infant Teacher Extraordinaire and Nice Girl, who will go on from one success to another for the rest of her lucky life. Bunyan would have no knowledge of this type, and Drabble is slightly skeptical about her ("O almost confident apostrophe" [153]). For one influenced by the evangelical tradition, such ease must seem a rebuke of hard work and difficulty.

One way of accepting such facility is not to take it very seriously. Drabble might dose herself and the reader with a bit of sly self-mockery or an intrusive narrator, techniques she could have found in *The Pilgrim's Progress,* whose narrator intrudes through a dream framework that relates to real events (e.g., Bunyan's imprisonments). In part 1, Bunyan actually becomes the mediator of his characters' experiences for the audience. Much has, of course, been made of autobiographical elements in Drabble's novels as well as of the presumptuous narrative presence in most of them. More could, no doubt, be made of her own Freudian interests, of the self-revealing nature of her fiction, and of the fact that she is a serious person/ writer who wants to be taken seriously but cannot quite take herself so. Possibly Drabble, attracted to Bunyan, parodied—because she could not take herself so seriously—his narrative style in some of her earlier works, then dropped the parody when she wrote her first greatly serious novel, whose third-person narration expands only to let us inside Rose and Simon. Not that Bunyan is without humor. Puns, double entendres, and quibbles abound in his writings; and he felt his verbal dexterity a part of the "mind-work" that facilitates the study of scripture. Drabble shapes her heroine's life with the needle passage and the Bunyan-sounding word *yonder* that fascinates Rose and Joyce and lets Emily pun on *vest* (226). The librarian who thinks *Animal Farm* a zoology textbook (138–39) and the woman who took home the *Gnomes of Zurich* for her children are piquantly humorous. Similarly, Rose believes that the Greek woman whose husband has died is talking about the weather when she points to heaven. Unlike Bunyan, Drabble uses such verbal artifice to measure the difficulty of communicating among even the most well-intended.

The woman behind the grill of the post-office window (137), a would-be center of communication, becomes a variation on Bunyan's "man in the iron cage." Rose leads the queued "congregation" in the only reasonable response to the woman's recalcitrance, laughter, an antidote loosed in the sleep of Bunyan's elect pilgrims. The scenes in the Interpreter's House are often such "moving" emblematic scenes, but Bunyan uses more ordinary ones and contributed a children's book to the emblem tradition. The adaptations of emblem in *The Needle's Eye,* for example, the peppered moth and the London Rocket, an herb, figure forth survival.

Inequality

"The Gifts of War." Drabble did not take her theme of inequality and privilege from Bunyan's elect and damned or from the feminist movement. Her privileged are oddities in recognizing their good fortune and luck and worrying about those who lack them. Even in *The Needle's Eye,* however, where the focus is on the relationship between riches and privilege and where Rose's concern for others is paramount, Drabble does not get inside the heads of those who lack privilege. They are present but only through the liberal humanitarianism that demarks most of the main characters. This void is filled by an exceptional short story published two years before *The Needle's Eye.*

"The Gifts of War" (1970) is about the "immeasurable gap of quality"[9] between the lives of the unnamed woman in the first section and of Frances Janet Ashton Hall in the second, despite the fact that they have been brought up in the same part of England. Frances is an "ardent" pacifist. A true Drabble woman, she is introspective and, like Rose, carries on a "dialogue with her own conscience" (30), centering on whether she is "doing the right thing but for the wrong reason." During this Easter, is she wearing her sandwich-board more for peace in Vietnam and a banning of all armaments or for the sake of Michael Swaines, a "swain"? She may get "a sort of corrupt pleasure in doing things she didn't like doing . . . when she knew that it was being appreciated by other people: a kind of yearning for disgrace and martyrdom" (30). Rose does not like the public features of her role and is a very poor speaker, but her motivation is pure self-abnegation. Moreover, Frances's wish that the protests could be "sociable" parodies the emphasis on communality in *The Needle's Eye.*

The woman finds her identity as Kevin's "Mum." Her life has, but for him, ground down to a dim survival level. Once one of a tram of "Betty Joneses," she had no money but was "still hopeful, still endowed with the touching faith that . . . deliverance would be granted to her in the form of money, marriage, romance, [or a] visiting prince . . ." (26). Marriage was a false deliverance, a Bunyanesque "mire" "of penury and beer and butchery" (28).

The woman's emblem is the willowherb, which, in still more foreshadowings of *The Needle's Eye,* grows on bombed sites and in thin soil. It symbolizes her son, her escape and "election," and makes her "almost visionary" (28), like Rose and Simon, and ultimately is the index to human survival, as the bay tree is at the end of *The Middle Ground.* Not that this salvation has been without pain. The birth of Kevin was horrible (28); even now, like Rosamund's "millstone," the maternal role is "her joy, her sorrow," and the oxymoronic nature of their relationship (23, 25) becomes a comment on life at its best. Kevin gives her a "way of accepting, without too much submission, her lot" (21).

In the kind of Wordsworthian variation of which Drabble is fond, the "child is father of the husband." He play-acts with her the man-woman relationship (21) and gives her identity (22) in the eyes of the neighborhood from whom pride keeps her separated. In the image Drabble usually reserves for the soul, he reminds her of a bird (24) and renews the soul in her. They enjoy "lovely moment[s] of grace" (23), though she knows all the while that his excluding her to go along to school with a friend portends the greater separation to come. Yet in willing herself to forget his "adoring infancy," avoiding his touch and making herself satisfied with the "more familiar" "hostilities between them" (23), she lives the separation before it comes. Again, will and strain tell. She lacks flexibility and locks herself away behind one expression (25).

Drabble's epigraph for "The Gifts of War" comes from book 2 of Virgil's *Aeneid*, which recounts the fall of Troy triggered by the gift of the wooden horse. Latent in the story's title is the fact that Kevin is a gift of the "war" between his mother and father as well as a literal reference to the fact that she is on her way to town to buy the "pointless gift" (25) he has requested for his birthday, a toy Desperado Destruction Machine that is a "gift" of the war in Vietnam. The war of the story is also the distance between the classes represented by the woman and Frances. Frances and Michael assail her in the toy department where she goes to make her purchase and try to convince her that her gift will be harmful. They unwittingly make her believe she was on the verge of becoming a Judas by using her hoarded thirty shillings to betray the one person she loves in all the world.

Frances cannot know what has happened to this woman who has found one way, Kevin, her "salvation" (27), to endure her life. The girl is on "the verge of escape" (29) from this provincial world with a university degree in economics. Kevin has kept the woman from sinking to the level of existence imposed by her world. She sinks when, in total despair, she looses the obscenity that demarks the world of which she is now a part. Yet the process has only been hastened. The woman has mistakenly assumed her case unique whereas most mothers in the Drabble world feel her way about most children. With a glimmer of insight, she has attempted to stanch the wounds of coming separation and of her life in general by submitting to hardness and difficulty now. By pretending that only these exist, she does not tempt fate to crush out the life she has made for herself and her son.

There is no one to tell the woman that she is not unique. In contrast, Frances's parents have told her that what she and Michael are doing is wrong. Frances also remembers the short story by Saki, "The Toys of Peace," "about the impossibility of making children play with anything but soldiers" (32). Lacking such stays as parental advice and literature, the woman will never be able to cross the barriers of privilege. More horrible is the fact that Frances, for all her aids and "sense of social responsibility" (32), cannot enter the woman's world.

"**Homework.**"   In "Homework," a later short story, inequality
is still the focus, but much less overtly. The little piece might well
have been included in chapter 3 with other "female success stories"
except that the narrator is not the successful one of the two women
who are presented. Moreover, she is oblivious of the problems of
containment her nameless friend faces.

The first-person narrator, Meg, details a domestic conflict between a friend and her son Damie, who wants help with his homework. At first, she merely tells him to "bugger off,"[10] but when
he persists, on the last occasion knocking over the table lamp she
has just been repairing, she flies into a rage, throws objects at Damie,
and shouts abuse until he retreats. Meg tries to make peace but is
rebuffed and leaves. When she comes back to look in the window,
she sees the mother and son on the settee "hugging each other and
laughing their heads off" (13) and cannot imagine what they could
find amusing.

Meg's gibes tell us more about her than her friend, who is a
successful career woman putting in long days at work. Meg is
spinsterish, though, like her roommate Mary, she could be separated
from a husband or divorced. She may well have lived with her father
until he went into an Old People's Home. She is currently having
problems with Mary, who has talked her into putting a deposit on
a cottage for Easter and then reneged. Of course, that money would
not cause a moment's worry for her hostess, but not everybody is
that "rich" (11).

Meg is a classic, one of those people, too often women, who have
mastered the arts of condemning as they praise and of self-serving
with each utterance: her friend is "very generous"; "You're the busy
one, not me, I'm nobody, I always say: just you give me a ring if
you can't manage Tuesday, we can easily fix another day. I'm *always*
free" (7). While she would not be a nuisance for the world, she
does sometimes wonder about all the interruptions that happen
during her weekly visits.

Her friend is a busy woman who uses bad language; is "incapable
. . . of just sitting down and doing nothing" (10); lets her four
children make too much noise and watch too much television; allows
her eight-year-old twins, her youngest, to be too "precocious"; serves
only fruit and cheese instead of a real dessert; listens "with half an
ear" (11); is not very good at being helped but had "rather do things
herself" (8); drinks too much; and plays up the image of being a

"working mother," a "superwoman," and a "capable woman we're all supposed to think is such a model of efficiency and calm" (12). She has an ex-husband, who is responsible for one of the interrupting phone calls that delay dinner and to whom she speaks in "that special brisk tone" (9) Kate uses with her ex-lover in *The Middle Ground*. Meg is certain it conceals pain.

These two women are certainly not equals, but for none of the reasons Meg supposes. The differences in economic and career status are of little consequence. Nor is childlessness the sole cause for the lack of empathy. Meg's inability to give a name to the friend throughout her rambling narrative suggests her very real jealousy and solipsism and prepares us to believe that she secretly takes delight in the woman's fall from grace. These flaws dull her natural instincts, and she misses the irony of their discussion of Mary: "Yes it's amazing how insensitive people can be, she said . . ." (9).

Meg has no conception of the discipline required of her friend to work all day and then do "home work" that includes catering to Meg, one of the world's "unlovely" people. When the friend, no doubt at another rope's end, lightly suggests a psychiatrist, the hint is ignored. At the end, hurt by her brusque dismissal, however, Meg perverts the advice and concludes that the friend is "a little unbalanced" and needs "treatment" (13). Males are not the only villains in Drabble's world.

Males in Drabble's Novels

While *The Needle's Eye* is the first novel to give a male character equal status, Drabble was always uneasy about her portrayal of men. In "The Gifts of War," the wife is also culpable in the ruined marriage (e.g., 21). In *A Summer Bird-Cage*, Stephen has no redeeming features, Francis is "enchanting," and John is neutral. We have little opportunity to judge for ourselves, and Halifax remains one of the novel's flaws. In *The Garrick Year*, David and Wyndham chill until we realize Emma's own flaws. The exceptional male is Julian, who, with Stephen in *The Realms of Gold*, explodes the stereotype of female neurosis. Stephen and Phillipa Denham suggest cosmic aberration. The novels thus display a mixed, not strictly developmental approach to the males and interchange human problems among males and females, leaving behind the feminine survey of the earlier books that helped Drabble write easily what she knew.

Hamish, Joe, Roger, and George in *The Millstone* are manipulated by Rosamund and kept at a distance from us. The "common otherness" she learns through Octavia applies to men only in the remote abstract. She remains the "cold fish" type that Simon in *The Needle's Eye* only appears to be. Indeed, Drabble remains very much aware of her shortcomings; and in *The Middle Ground,* Rosamund is perhaps about to get her comeuppance by becoming involved with Ted the womanizer.

Jerusalem the Golden is the first novel to get inside the head of a man. Limited and terse (162–69), the portrayal of Gabriel is among Drabble's best, whether of male or female, and ranks with the incisive presentation of the nameless woman in "The Gifts of War." Gabriel bears the clear stamp of the analytic Drabble female, indeed plays that role because the heroine, Clara, cannot. Despite his sexuality and handsomeness, Drabble draws attention to his double nature when Clara thinks he has a girl's name (140). His fears could be expressed by a female. His male boss is in love with him and urges him to work before the cameras, but Gabriel wants to be "more than a pretty face" (139) and is afraid that people will tire of him.

Gabriel is also typical in his seeming privilege. His "strict inheritance" (166) makes him doubt the worth of his profession and project on his parents a condemnation of his "easy life" (138). Gabriel, who, Clara is sure, has come to lead her to heaven, knows he is "well-equipped" and "favourably singled out by destiny" (167), but his "sense of luck and destiny" has been "steadily eroded by years of disastrous marriage" (162). Rejected by Phillipa, he knows that "he was about to kiss somebody" (162) when Clara appeared.

Like other Drabbleans, Gabriel suspects that his failure with Phillipa is a "saving lack of grace" that prevents his life from being too golden; "without it he would have been more surely ruined" (167). He is disgusted with himself not for failing but for having tried over the years to conceal the truth about her trauma from the neighbors, yet gives much of his life to hoping that he and their marriage are not responsible for her mental damage. He recalls incidents to make his "heart bleed" (164) when his tenderness for her lapses and feels guilty about his relationship with his parents and siblings.

Gabriel endures. He puts up with the condition of the house and tries to humor and help his wife as best he can. Humanized by his horrible marriage, his dislike of his work because he has to please too many people, his sense that no one with three children can avoid being poor, and his vulnerability, Gabriel is a triumph. He will not turn his face to the wall or be paralyzed by inequality as is Phillipa, who cannot "bear to have more of anything than anyone in the world" and to whom misery seems a "duty" (165).

Gabriel reappears with a new wife in *The Middle Ground* and is still having domestic difficulties. Jessica believes he is having an affair with Kate while he is actually having one ("if so it could be called" [217]) with his research assistant. He and Kate have had a long friendship and are now working together on "Women at the Crossroads." Acceptable as an individual, Gabriel, once in a group of men, is not to be trusted to consider women rightly. He is yet a prey to his image; he is "all that men might be," and even a "hostile husband" dare not treat him "with anything other than respect" (205). And he is still horrified by Phillipa, who has become "a devout Catholic convert, and a visitor of the dying" (198).

In *The Waterfall,* James, if a bit freakish, is reminiscent of Francis in *A Summer Bird-Cage.* The remote but tortured and driven Malcolm, whose life Jane makes miserable, shares with Sarah and many Drabble females a penchant for justifying life by its level of difficulty.

Although critics are unsympathetic to Simon of *The Needle's Eye,* he is at least as complex and soul-driven as Rose. As if to submerge sexual stereotypes forever, Drabble creates him passive to Rose's active. He knows that he ought to force her to run with him for freedom, but he cannot act or will a response: "He was not good at responses, so many had he of necessity curbed" (75).

Hugh, Frances's brother in *The Realms of Gold,* is a "golden boy" manqué, as some of Drabble's females occasionally fear that they are women manqué. Karel is the archetypal victim of his own good nature, with the doubleness of his name a possible cue that this role has here passed from Woman. By Drabble's own admission, David was intended to play a larger role but became "impenetrable" (152)— perhaps because he was to have been a kind of "golden boy" re-placement for Hugh and a complement to Frances. He is the only major character in Drabble, male or female, to suffer a complete breakdown.

Anthony, of *The Ice Age,* is similar to Simon in *The Needle's Eye.* He has more claim to being Drabble's protagonist than Alison and is the true mothering figure of the novel, taking on the responsi-

bilities not only for her two children but for the condition of England
and the world. Detractors may argue that Drabble is subconsciously
stereotyping in choosing a male lead for the first novel to center on
universal problems, but she can counter with the role reversing in
The Ice Age and with the fact that Alison precedes Anthony in world
probing. We are also allowed inside the heads of lower-class Len
and Maureen, whose cogent portrayals deny sexual inequality.

The Middle Ground, as if to suggest that Drabble has nothing left
to prove about her handling of men cuts back to a female protagonist.
Kate is surrounded, with the exception of Hugo, by largely stereotypic males: Stuart, who may be homosexual; fat, jealous Peter,
who writes her anonymous letters; the once powerful Hunt, now a
hanger-on of her circle; womanizing Ted Stennett; Mujid the for-
eigner; and Joseph Leroy, the Rastafarian (whose last name Drabble
surely did not mean to make so stereotypic as it is!). In a sense,
the novel is a throwback: Kate is a woman trying to find out who
she is. Though middle-aged and successful, she is bored and ready
to question her gains. Her story is a variation on Homer's *Odyssey,*
with this Penelope trying to keep faith with the identity she finds.
The men, not all suitors, nonetheless want something from her,
and she is also probing what she has to give.

We can scarcely doubt that Drabble wanted to prove she could
depict men. The point is that, in terms of the kinds of problems
they face, they quickly became interchangeable with her women.
The important growth may be from her characters, male and female,
trying to find out who they are to trying to find out how they relate
to other people.

"Hassan's Tower." Drabble's first presentation of a man's point
of view occurs in "Hassan's Tower" (1966), a microcosm of the
Drabble world. Kenneth achieves a sense of relation not only to his
wife of two weeks but to humanity. He and Chloe reassert the theme
of privilege through money. She has always been from the "right"
class and has inherited wealth. He is a writer earning shocking sums
for work he cannot take seriously. A true Drabblean introspective,
he worries about his own "meanness" and inexperience, interpreting
Chloe's every nuance as a mark of her class but irritated when she
fails to enact its stereotypes. Their class differences are mirrored in
the Moroccans and make "his head split in efforts of comprehension."[11] Now blind to Tangier's beauty, he supposes his vision ruined
by money and despises himself.

Self-dissatisfaction turns outward to Chloe, whom he now feels he married from a sense of pathos and obligation. On such a dim note, they creak through the honeymoon, going at length, by accident or fate, to Rabat where they eat in a restaurant named for the landmark "Hassan's Tower," which Chloe must see despite his complaint of holiday crowds. Younger, she is rapt at its view while his spirits are "unbelievably low from some dreadful bleak sightless premonition of middle age" (53). In a typical Drabble image, Kenneth tries to deal with the "stony problem" (54) of his marriage. They were passionate once, but he has finished with love as with scenery and must be content with the rare privilege of having known both. He resolves, Atlas-like, to endure, and shortly uses Bunyan's "burden" motif (56).

Kenneth's whining-become-insight remains hard to accept: "when the brightness of illumination" fades, he will have "the faith and grounds of knowledge" (58–59). Drabble published her book on Wordsworth in the same year as this short story and surely had in mind his acceptance of the adult's diminished power to feel and discover human and natural beauty, but we have difficulty acknowledging Kenneth's worthiness to have the moment of illumination (in the standard Drabble image of a bird [58]) in Hassan's tower, the complement of Wordsworth's Alps.

"Hassan's Tower" is a miniature of Drabble's theme of community. In Kenneth's vision, the world is no longer empty, and foreigners cease to be foreigners (59). The natives become individuals: "They were many and various, and because they were many and various they were one, and he was admitted" (58). "Hassan's Tower" has most in common with *The Needle's Eye* and thus also aptly shares Bunyan's vision of the diversity of humanity.

"Crossing the Alps." The same communal vision is gained by Daniel ("Crossing the Alps," 1969), for whom everything has also gone awry. He and his mistress, drawn together through misery, have managed a week of freedom to drive to Yugoslavia. Her "burdens," the Bunyanesque image employed in the story,[12] are "the dotty mother, the cruelly defective child, the cruelly defected husband" (195); his, a frigid and hysterical wife with a taste for gloom. Providence conspires to give him the flu, and he enumerates all the mishaps that may prevent their escape. His "feminine" sensibilities range from urging her to the safe, "confined space" of the car (154) to fearing that she is "sick of the sight of him" and is not waiting "with an anxiety equal to his own, to feel his arms around her yet again" (194). He is protective not only because she has once tried to gas herself and the child but because he believes in and admires, with most of Drabble's characters, survival and endurance. His own shameful interest in food seems to make him not serious enough to deserve her.

Drabble again introduces role reversal as Daniel, accustomed to shoring up her flagging spirits, becomes helpless because of his illness and the concomitant change she undergoes. Driving and making decisions, she seems "larger" and assumes an "extra quality" (195) while he is left in the car like a sleeping child. He reassumes some control by forcing her to tears through his despair at their hopelessness: no good can come of their being "so kind and careful" (197).

Out of such recognition and resolve, both salvage something, but Daniel takes the true spoils of the journey: a "mystic sense of the unity of all sorrow" (198). To arrive there, he has, though half-delirious, done Bunyan's "mind work" in response to the woman's complaint against nature's "nothingness, without people" (196), an echo of Emma in *The Garrick Year*. As Daniel ponders her charge, he throws up Bunyan's merging of natural and spiritual topography: "those vast moving shapes and abrupt inclines and icy summits were . . . emblems of conditions . . ." (196). Her observation occurs when she has pulled the large car off the road in the "vast presence of mountains" and in a landscape recalling the central episode of *The Waterfall*. Drabble rounds out the story with verification of the Wordsworth epigraph. Years later, the thought of pine trees or Alpine landscapes reminds Daniel "of something half realized, a revelation of comfort too dim to articulate, a revelation that had lost its words and its fine edges and its meaning but not its images." Drabble's favored share Wordsworth's belief in infinitude, hope, effort, desire, and expectation—"something evermore about to be."

Chapter Six

Marriage

The Garrick Year

The second novel, *The Garrick Year* (1964), is the only one to focus entirely on marriage. More tautly constructed than *A Summer Bird-Cage,* it centers on Emma Evans's survival of a seven-month "exile" from London. Her husband, David, a successful television actor, receives a plum: the opportunity to perform legitimate theater in Hereford under the direction of the famous Wyndham Farrar. The problem is that Emma, the first-person narrator and a model before her four-year-old marriage, has been offered a job as a part-time television news announcer. It would take her away only a few nights a week and thus would let her have and enjoy everything: a career, marriage, and her children, Flora and Joseph, the latter only seven weeks old. Argument, spite, and silent fury are of no avail with her husband; Emma must derive what satisfaction she can from playing the martyr.

Emma's plight echoes her creator's. Drabble left Cambridge with scholarly and acting accolades to become the wife of an actor with the Royal Shakespeare Company. In Stratford, her "Hereford," she understudied or played bit parts, later waited in a dressing room with her son,[1] heard about the dangers of the river, and read about two drownings. Her recourse was to "exorcise her fears" for Adam in her fiction (Creighton, 24).

Emma goes to Hereford with her husband but is not quiescent in spite of her claim that stoicism is the only answer for the deprivations (e.g., independence, hope, and expectation [10]) marriage has wrought. When she meets the cast on the train to Hereford, she records Sophy Brent's dismissal of her as just a mother and sets out to prove her underestimation. One method to this end is her outlandish appearance at the civic reception for the acting company. She continues to do the unexpected and to be unsubdued by transport to the country.

Emma likes controversy for its own sake and its sharpening of her faculties and secretly looks upon the journey as an opportunity. She primes herself for the experience but admits nothing so comforting to David. "Full of buds and nervous colour, after [her] impersonal childbearing winter," she anticipates finding "an enemy, a lover, or that somebody like myself that I see once a year in the back of a passing taxi or drawing the curtains of an upstairs room" (52–53).

She finds the lover in Wyndham, who does not remember their meeting at a London party when she was pregnant. She was also on the cover of a magazine that reviewed one of his plays. Their first Hereford encounter occurs in the theater when she has made a domestic foray to relieve her boredom. He finds her standing before a bulletin board placing push pins in the circle that symbolizes the closed quality of her life. She is attracted because he speaks to her as a person and not to David's wife or to a woman "who seemed from the eccentricity of her hair style to be an actress" (95). As a result, she forgets her tin of oil, though she does not usually forget anything. Like other Drabble women, Emma loves travel and cars and is responsive when Farrar gestures to her from his Jaguar. Chance encounters culminate in their being trapped together during a power failure, a symbolic warning. When he drives her into Wales, where she has never been despite David's being Welsh, they nearly have a wreck, and she establishes her policy of allowing no petting below the waist. The affair would not have been consummated but for Emma's finding David with Sophy and feeling indebted to Wyndham for putting up with her. He represents little more to her than zestful change, and, despite his womanizing, he is drawn to her for reasons other than sex. When he learns of the plane crash killing the American benefactress who has built the theater and sponsored the festival, he calls Emma for advice.

In Hereford, Emma has taken the role of mother lightly, leaving the children to the care of the French maid, Pascal. As if to recall her to her duties, while she is in the park with Wyndham, Flora falls in the Wye. Emma immediately goes to her rescue, and the fright of threatened loss pulls David and her together again. To give Emma time to recuperate from the experience and her cold, David takes the children and Pascal out. Emma lets Wyndham into her bed as enthusiastically as Rose her Czechoslovakian. Afterward, she blows her nose in her pillow and ends the affair. As she directs

Wyndham's backing out of the garage, he runs into her and hurts her legs. During her recovery, she and David forgive each other's trespasses.

The community of family is reachieved during a country outing comparable to the picnic by the sea in *The Needle's Eye*. When Flora encounters a quiescent sheep, only Emma sees the real snake clutching its belly: " 'Oh well, so what,' is all that one can say, the Garden of Eden was crawling with [snakes], too, and David and I managed to lie amongst them for one whole pleasant afternoon. One just has to keep on and to pretend, for the sake of the children, not to notice" (255).

The novel as novel.   *The Garrick Year* is often praised, and an excerpt has been used to exemplify "character and manners" in modern fiction.[2] Its control and plot are strong, and it is permeated by the spirit of the theater and could be easily dramatized. The limited number of characters is gathered to perform a repertory of plays in the provinces. The title reinforces the theatrical content, for Mrs. Von Blerke believes herself related to the eighteenth-century actor, Hereford-born David Garrick; it also prognosticates since Garrick's own Stratford jubilee was a fiasco largely because of the flooding of the Avon.

Emma's flashback is triggered by seeing Sophy in a television commercial, and there are more true "incidents" and less of the purely anecdotal than in most Drabble novels. They are the discovery of Sophy and David, the accident with the gas while Emma is out with Wyndham, Emma's rescue of Flora from the Wye, the consummation of Emma's affair, Wyndham's backing into Emma with his car, the suicide of Julian, and the family picnic. Below the surface, the novel is a self-exploration for Emma, an attempt to move toward acceptance of a life that has turned out to be quite different from the one she anticipated; marriage, if not Emma, triumphs. The book is also controlled by image chains that provide insight into her personality: violence, water, cars, and machinery.

Many of the names are suggestive. The heroine recalls Jane Austen's Emma Woodhouse and Gustave Flaubert's Emma Bovary. Other writers are remembered in Emma's maiden name, Lawrence, and in Pascal. Emma ferrets out the information that Farrar has been named for Wyndham Lewis. "Mary Scott" has historical echoes and has in fact majored in history. David is aptly named to honor Garrick and, a Welshman, has some of the flamboyance of Dylan

Thomas and Richard Burton. His last name suggests another the-atrical pillar, Dame Edith Evans. The saving of "Flora" reveals that Emma is a more "natural" mother and is more in consonance with nature than she claims.

The Garrick Year **and the woman theme.** Many critics con-sider this novel feminist,[3] and Drabble says Emma "went off wildly as soon as those children were off at school" (Hardin, 281). "Wildly" is the cue. *The Garrick Year* is about coming to grips with life. Emma has to be calm or give the nursing baby wind. Mary's and her paths have reversed. Emma, the daughter of a Cambridge don, was expected to be the career woman, but she went to Italy and has "done nothing at all" (109). Mary attended a university and then took a diploma of education. Emma gets no comfort from her modeling, the product of her looks; like Gabriel Denham, she feels guilty about her facility. News reporting would have proved her worth.

In a classic Drabble image, Emma feels her *self* stretch and "put out damp, bony wings"; she is a "hungry bony bird" "ready for some unexplained famine to eat straw and twigs and paper" (131–32). She has become a wife and mother before knowing who she is, but David has become an actor, a husband, and a father without knowing who he is either. Julian, unable to be the kind of actor his father expects or to accept his homosexuality, drowns himself. Throughout her sojourn in Hereford, Emma observes others, males and females, trying to make their ways, living the ways they have chosen, or succumbing before the effort. She sees license versus rigidity in Sophy and Mary (114) and life as a discipline versus life as an entertainment in Mike and Wyndham (154–55). The dangers of living at the extremes of the continuum, as well as her own indecisiveness and doubts, are shown in her dream about Julian, "his thin girl's body . . . so different from Wyndham's solid trunk or David's muscular torso" (232), and in her ultimate recognition of her wrong-dealing with Wyndham: "I had opened myself either too little or too much, I had not faced the choice that I should have faced and I had ended up with neither infidelity nor satisfaction" (243). What she has ended up with is life, at best an oxymoron, "quiet discontented pleasure" (222).

Expectations founder for all. Sophy, unable to accept the fact that she is a poor actress, pretends success. Wyndham's sister, having married wealth, intended to devote her life to assisting her brother, but he does not need her. Wyndham lessons Emma about the illusory nature of success: "I used to think . . . that nothing could be worse than wanting something and not getting it . . . , but I don't see things that way any more. The more I do, the more limitations I find in myself, the happier I am. I've got to like it, the warm cozy feeling of defeat" (187). Drabble brings them to parody when Emma's "terrific breasts" (170) shrink after she weans Joseph, and Wyndham playfully accuses her of deceiving him. If Emma laments her descent to the washing machine (158–59), Mrs. Von Blerke drowns during the realization of her greatest dream.

Emma's relationship with Wyndham, sought to escape boredom, ironically makes time "thick" (164). Her being twenty-six to his forty-three accounts for only some of the disparity in their viewpoints, and she is responsive to his changing "expectations" as he records Binneford House shrinking when he was seventeen and growing again (170) after the war. Wyndham, too, has some blind spots and vows never again to love a woman with children (252).

Emma tends to blame her dissatisfaction on David and her children, but she has helped make marriage a Bunyanesque "muddy hill of domination" (19). She not only pretends to protest David's touch but has conceived her children "by force" (89). As rigid as Rosamund Stacey, she divides the world into those with and without children (51) and women into professionals and nonprofessionals (74); "we are what we seem to be" (238), she says, and so becomes an adulteress.

Emma is *in marriage* what she was *before marriage*. She has always been dissatisfied, even as a school girl awaiting something exciting. Another Drabblean, she likes journeys, stations, trains, and cars— emblems of change and possibility. Like David, Wyndham feeds her need for aberration. His gesturing from his big car is a replay of her encounter with David on a train. Marrying was "the most frightful, unlikely thing" she could do; life with David "might be a nightmare, an adventure, but whatever else exciting . . . he would go at life hard, with his head down and his fists clenched, forever. I did not want an easy life, I wanted something precipitous . . ." (33). Their marriage is threaded on a string of small violences, shocking and pleasing to both. Crisis is defused when he beats a hole in the wall with his fist. In Hereford, he anticipates Rose Vassiliou by heaving Emma's marble pillar down the garage stairs. She is still attracted by his studied insults and his deliberate hurting of people he does not like. Farrar's kindred perverseness (e.g., leaving the woman who expected him to change fuses) allures.

Emma has always been lured by the freakish. Propriety is redeemed by the drawer of junk in the bottom of the Scotts' wardrobe. She likes "nothing new that is not monstrous" (39) and prefers hors d'oeuvres to main courses (188). She deliberately swam out of her depths for "the fright of it": "The empty water, simply because it was empty water, was what I wanted: empty water, no matter how far down you reach, and no foothold" (116). She wants life to be governed by accidents (39) and ignores the warnings (e.g., the broken teapot) that she must not rebel against her fate. Yet she compares the sensation of the car against her legs with that of a person drowning (246). Her daughter is a surrogate for her in the Wye, a culmination of Emma's literal and figurative swimming out of her depths. Mrs. Von Blerke and Julian are also surrogates, and they die. Emma feels for that "dead wet lady, who floated from some fishlike watery depths of coincidence across the trivial sentimental drama of [her] life" (152), but only much later does she exchange coincidence for fate: "nothing is trivial, there is a providence, as the Bible says, in the fall of a sparrow" (251).

Emma is the product of her parents and environment. Her father is a theologian, who, with the delicacy of his class, has not imposed his ways on her. Her mother, who died at age forty-three of tuberculosis, drank and left her to a nanny. While she does not necessarily give us the truth about herself (Creighton, 22), we deduce that the lack of definition at home has shaped her need for delineation. The theological discussions she hears never resolve anything. Left with a passion for facts, she types lists about the Angevin Empire and, while feeding Joseph, learns dates related to the Sicilian Vespers. Accordingly, she is not susceptible to symbol and, at eleven, determines that "poetry is one thing and living another" (118). "Real conflict" for her is "wordless," and she finds "drama and the theatre so unreal" (220). She detests the theoretical discussions of the actors and rejoices in the conversation of Papini— "like a Cambridge discussion, after weeks of messy latitude" (148).

In *A Summer Bird-Cage*, Sarah resents the "formlessness" of women. Emma, ironically ignoring the form imposed on her life by marriage and motherhood, detests David's formlessness: he "has no more self than a given quantity of water and . . . is always trying to contain his own flowing jelly-like shapelessness in some stern mould or confine because he is . . . afraid of the aimlessness of his own undirected violence" (84). He is a coward because he finds "a sense of clarity, a feeling of being, by words and situations not of his own making, defined and confined, so that his power and his energy could meet together in one great explanatory moment" (160–61). While recognizing how alike they are (28), Emma does not admit her self-contradictoriness. She wants to have both ends of the continuum—definition and aberration. She is contemptuous of David's unconventional profession and at the same time of its ability to give shape through its characters. Yet the facts she memorizes are not her own, and newscasting would have had her reading others' words. Emma's "soul's in a bad way" (233) long before David and the children. If her mind has "munching jaws" (105) and is a "furtive hutch" (162), she must feed it instead of taking out her misery on her husband. She emits unwitting sense in her "but for the rubbish that I carried along with me in my mind I was as free as anyone to go anywhere" (165).

What Emma learns. Emma does not sing aloud the nursery song that keeps coming into her head after Flora escapes the Wye. It is a dialogue between a mother and daughter, who is allowed to "go out to swim" so long as she does not "go near the water." In the second verse, she can go if the boys do not see her get in, if she will "keep right under the water" (227). To Emma, the song seems "appropriate to something: to marriage, perhaps, or the emancipation of women" (228). Life is such a conundrum but must be coped with. Her marriage may lack meaning from moment to moment, but she learns that it has meaningfulness. In her pursuit of Wyndham, she thinks herself apart from David and the children, but she has moments of insight. Watching Flora play with David, she feels "from a long way off an immense forgiveness of him and hope for forgiveness from him; nothing near, nothing present, but the awareness of some distant factual understanding, as though I knew him too well not at some point to sympathize with what he was feeling" (163–64). They have a small reconciliation when she admits to more between them "than a wardrobe" (59). They pass the Drabble test of mutual commitment by making the same statement when she finds him with Sophy, a symbolic putting aside of their individuality for what they are as man and wife. They are struck by the "terrifying unison" of their parental response to Flora (227), and Wyndham flees before it. Thinking back over the Garrick year, Emma may see further into their relationship. In the course of her story, she is clearly far more mother than wife, a fact effectively highlighted by her calling her husband "Dave" once, when he describes taking Flora out after her accident.

Marriage is unsavory in Drabble, but the reasons can be traced in the characters. Wyndham's "people who get married give up the here and now for the sake of the hereafter" (238) is wrong but no more so than Emma's identification of love with babies (194) to the exclusion of their fathers. The fact that her visit to Wyndham's apartment is a miniature of her domestic doldrums must make her think. She and David have gone into marriage fighting each other rather than pulling together to fight the stereotype of marriage. He rails against her wasting money and pretends to read her mail and make decisions without consulting her. She does go through his mail and pretends to hate being taken to Hereford while avidly devouring everything she can about Garrick. She blames David for the loss of "wideness and sharpness" (135) in her conversation and expects to regain these arts with Wyndham, a name-dropper. With echoes of *A Summer Bird-Cage,* Emma knows she is "lucky" to have David and is restless because he is so handsome (68). The contrast between what she ought to feel and what she feels frustrates her. She complains about never having any time off from him (136) and makes "a principle of suiting [herself] rather than the children" (47). She forgoes some solipsism: "I would have to spend my life not in protecting myself but in protecting others from myself, starting with my children, and continuing with the rest of my acquaintance" (250–51).

Emma grows emotionally. Initially fascinated by machines, particularly cars, and tending toward mechanical images, she does not cry (21), but she comes to cry on several occasions during the Garrick year and for increasingly nonsolipsistic reasons. She is not, however, a cold person except to those she perceives as a threat to her identity. She is kind to Julian and is horrified at the way the acting company treats him, though we may infer more of Drabble's Freudianism here, since his lack of masculinity entices Emma, who would prefer to dispense with sex or let it proceed no further than the back-seat petting of a simpler era. His hopelessness appeals to her, and, when he sends Flora a large doll, Emma feels that she will cry. The doll symbolizes the childlike nature of Julian and, as Emma comes to realize, of herself, as well as the identity between mother and daughter and its near loss.

Emma's tears attest to her love for and dependence on David, which she has tried to deny by playing at being indifferent to him throughout the novel. The morning after she has found him with Sophy, she collapses in a "sea of grief" (217) and in domestic chaos relieved only by seeing the effect mirrored in her daughter. She escapes to the launderette to be "cheered by the presence of so much quiet mechanical activity" (218) but finds she is not to be let off. Coincidence plants Sophy there, and Emma experiences "absurd delighted malice" at her wash being dyed "a horrid muddy pink" (221).

When Emma reads about the air disaster, she sheds "tears of gratitude" (141) for the rescue of the little boy who will rejoin his mother in England. Her ability to cry for others' children and not just for Flora drowning or crying alone in the night redeems her. The children serve as a kind of bridge to wider concerns, but Emma weights parenthood too high and makes us want to declaim a better way (enjoying the marriage). The experience of the Garrick year is buttressed by some of Drabble's favorite reading matter: Wordsworth, Hume, and Victorian novels. The result is a pat, one-sentence summary of Emma's marriage from Hume citing the "feebleness of human infancy": "there must be a union of male and female for the education of the young, and . . . this union must be of considerable duration" (252–53).

Nonetheless, through literature, Emma's heart has leapt upward and outward. As a school girl, she rejected Tennyson's "Break, break, break" because everyone was affected by it; in that rejection, she was striking a blow "for the sake of human independence" (118). She also jeered at Wordsworth's early poems: "But now I do not laugh, I weep, real wet tears, the same tears that I shed over newspaper reports of air disasters, for they are as moving as air disasters, those poems, they have as high a content of uninflated truth. And I weep partly as an apology for my past ignorance, from which I might never have been rescued" (253). Again, she seems too pat; we hear not Emma but Drabble, whose book on Wordsworth could be so epitomized and all of whose novels are apologia for him. *The Garrick Year* is only Drabble's second novel. In that just-right image for Papini, it still has a somewhat "bare" and "reed-in-the-wind" quality. Yet its slight superficiality is countered by the Wordsworth-ian overlay of Emma's newfound knowledge.

The opposition between the city (particularly London) and the country is a frequent theme in Drabble's novels, and, typically, the characters who condemn or eschew the provincial have most to learn. Emma sees the provinces as "curiosities" only (14), while "London means everything" to her, both "noise and human beauty"; she is "not a one for the inhuman, and the thought of nature and the limited range of social patterns" in Hereford horrify her. She "would be lost out there with the cattle and the actors, lost and nothing" (22). Emma is too strong for the particular loss of self symbolized by Sophy's "tinselness," but she prefers its brittleness and distancing to the engulfment represented, for example, in the Mower or garden poems of Andrew Marvell. She is frightened at Binneford House with the Wye looming below it: "the silent insect-filled damp of the evening was quite foreign to me, quite beyond my control. There was nothing within reach that I understood. Here I was, in the midst of all the greenery that I had mocked at with my friends in London, and I was unnerved by it. It seemed more real than London, the river and the trees and the grass, so much profusion, so much of everything, and not a human being in reach, not a person to watch it" (169). Emma wants no one, particularly David, to know her. She has learned to detach herself "from any attempt at a group" (179). Her drive for singularity sets her off from other Drabble characters who dislike the provinces. London and the job she has lost represent the opportunity to be "thoroughly public and anonymous" (180) while Hereford is classified—"little disconnected cells, and within each cell . . . laws and habits and a prescribed language, and prescribed jokes" (179). She, on the other hand, would be defined only by her insusceptibility to definition.

Symbolically, Emma overcomes her dislike of the countryside when the family goes to Ewyas Harold Common, which Drabble may have chosen for "Common" and for the fact that Ewyas is "say we" spelled backwards. The Garrick year has certainly taught her to spend less time on the singular and more on the "common" or universal. Perhaps Emma has repulsed nature, too, because of a secret fear that she would learn about it what she learns: a "real snake" clutches the sheep's belly. The sight must be particularly discomfiting to one who cannot subscribe to the ethic of "Oh love, let us be true to one another. . . ."

More Drabbleanism.   Emma is in the Drabble mold of the bright and different young women who think that the world is or ought to be their oyster. More aggressive and feisty than most, she is unwilling to give ground without a struggle. Four years of marriage have not softened her harsh edges. The Garrick year forces concessions, but she never makes them graciously. She will spend the rest of her life doing what she must but clawing out for herself "a fly in amber, or a sour black walnut, or a dead brown rose" (134), images she uses for the "strange pickled charm" of her "first outing" with Wyndham. She will also continue to be the series of contradictions that characterizes the Drabble woman. She wants to be free but wants to bind her life into segments of meaning.

More muted in this book is the theme of inequality. David has been brought up in poverty; Emma, in comfort. He is extravagant; she displays the scrupulousness with money that demarks her class. She worries about employing Pascal and fastidiously refuses to invade her privacy, with near disastrous results. At the same time, Emma manifests little of the guilt associated with privilege in Drabble's novels. She has never lived anywhere "less than beautiful" (40). Their London house is "the right thing" (41) and has stone lions on either side of the front door, an anticipation of the symbolic contrast between Rose and her parents in *The Needle's Eye*. However, if Emma is thus juxtaposed with the Bryanstons, some of her latent humanity is also revealed. Her reasons for going to Hereford forecast Rose on Christopher: "I did not want to separate the children from their father; I did not want anyone to criticize David for leaving me; I did not want David to be alone in Hereford, not only because I knew that if he went without me he would never come back, but also because I knew that he, too, would be lonely" (25).

Drabble on Marriage

While *The Garrick Year* is the first novel with a married heroine, all of Drabble's books critique marriage in some degree. *A Summer Bird-Cage* is a variation on *Hamlet* as Sarah ostensibly wrestles with the problem of "to marry or not to marry." She is in love but is brightly cautious about the likely outcomes for her sense of person. In contrast, Emma acts as though she "should have known better" than to marry David and must spend the rest of her married life making up to her image of herself for the lapse. In *The Millstone*,

Rosamund willfully chooses spinsterhood; no man is going to get close to her. In *Jerusalem the Golden,* Clara would like to be married to Gabriel for the impression he makes and is oblivious of the fact that there are no happy marriages in her novel.

The protagonists in the early novels, despite Drabble's insistence that she is a prefeminist writer, have a strong sense of selfhood that sends them into or toward marriage primed for the martial stance. Emma and Rosamund place themselves on such guard that no man will break through to the rose garden completely. Sarah is healthier; she goes delicately toward Francis, but she goes. At the other end of the continuum is Jane in *The Waterfall,* who withdraws into herself and becomes a parody of the Emily Dickinson type. Her husband is victimized by her compulsive self-absorption. Drawn out by another near-parody, James as romantic lover, she forsakes her responsibilities to others and lets passion take her. The modern cataclysm—an automobile accident—and the incongruity between their passion and nature's sublime restore a degree of reason.

In *The Needle's Eye,* Rose and Christopher fall from passion but unite because they have struggled so hard for the right to marry. Vassiliou fights to keep the marriage intact largely because of its image value, a motivation also for Nick and Diana. Rose, like Emma, is fighting for her individuality. Both yield to marriage for some lofty reasons. Simon, on the other hand, is akin to Jane as he withdraws into a damaging passivity. In the course of the novel, he learns from Rose, and his marriage will be better, if still far from ideal, in the future.

The short stories also present a negative view of marriage. The exception is "A Voyage to Cythera," whose heroine witnesses the resolving of some momentary marital discord. The point is not that she is unmarried, however, but that she is a nonparticipant in life in general. The husband she observes is sympathetically presented, as is the male protagonist in "Crossing the Alps." Drabble does not blame only males for failed marriages. Nonetheless, some of them are great horrors, for example, the husbands in "A Day in the Life of a Smiling Woman" and "The Gifts of War." In "The Reunion," the marriages of the respective lovers, we infer, are all right. The pair merely wants change and excitement and seems rather silly. The marriage has already ended in "Homework," and the divisiveness results from Meg's inability to understand the life of her friend, the career woman. "Hassan's Tower" reveals a newly married couple sniping at each other out of fear of the commitment made. Far more important there is the narrator's coming to grips with life at an acceptable level of diminishment. Similarly, "A Success Story" speaks to Kathie's humanity generally. She is not married but lives comfortably if not very passionately with a man. Like many Drabble characters, she is finding out that it is all right to be what she is.

The centrality of marriage dissipates after the short stories and the first six novels. The main figures in the last three are middle-aged and divorced. In *The Realms of Gold,* Frances eventually achieves a happy life with Karel, but we are likely to question her choice. The pleasant-enough relationship of the lovers in *The Ice Age* is foreshortened as chance and fate take over and Anthony spins away faster and faster into the world that builds inside his own head. *The Middle Ground* presents Kate Armstrong trying to carry on after a husband and lovers and a career that has become boring. Whatever is just around the corner is unlikely to be another marriage.

Two happy marriages appear in miniature in *The Realms of Gold* and *The Ice Age,* and one of them is dissolved by a blow of fate. Frances assesses Harold Barnard as a man who does not complain (267) or condescend (267) and is instantly curious about his life and wife. They match her expectations of "what life ought to be like": "Nice people, pleased to see one, in a nice comfortable place. She shivered on the edge of perfectly enjoying a perfectly ordinary experience, a perfectly ordinary encounter, an event so rare . . ." (268). She concludes that the couple's success is due to Mary's confident sexuality, their working "hard at continuing to feel so pleased with one another," their seeming childlessness, or, especially, their luck (268–69).

In *The Ice Age,* Kitty and Max have a successful marriage until he is killed by a bomb in a restaurant where they are celebrating their ruby wedding anniversary. We know little about Max, but she is the great empathizer, "a living proof of the possibility of good nature" (15), "a wonderful woman and a wonderful mother" (123). She is not the typical Drabble woman, for she is too good, too perfect. We can almost hear Drabble saying that we ought not to look for marriages such as Kitty's because they rarely exist and, when they do, are apt to evoke random tragedy because they go against the natural order.

Janet Bird in *The Realms of Gold.* Marriage is bleakest in the account of Janet Bird in *The Realms of Gold.* Like Emma, she has

been married four years and cannot understand why she married at
all; she has never loved Mark. The one year she was on her own
working was the best of her life. Yet some problems are of her own
making. Unlike Frances, who copes with the Ollerenshaw legacy
of depression by work, she walls herself off from others though she
does not give in to a childhood inclination toward suicide. At the
end of the book, despite her relationship with Frances, she refuses
to talk about her marriage problems and is "biding her time" (307).

Janet is in danger of being a type, as Frances suggests: "she knew
all too many people like Janet, tight-mouthed, slightly sour, over-
tidy . . . critical, mean, not yet quite hardened into irremediable
bitterness, but well on the way toward it" (273). Her last name,
"Bird," reminds us of Drabble's image for vulnerability. Janet rails
at herself for having been taken in by wedding presents and gives
Drabble occasion to expatiate playfully on the "tribal insanity" that
anesthetizes even sensible women about to be married "against self-
sacrifice" (107–8).

Until Frances, Janet's only solace is baby Hugh, who came late
and accidentally. Mark's source of sexual knowledge is sly, nasty
jokes, and Janet's instincts have taken them as far as they have gone.
She has become increasingly adept at the rhetoric of sexual avoidance.
Nor does she take naturally to mothering. The vicar is no answer
because he can change neither Mark, her, Tockley, nor their life
there. Besides, in the flatlands there are no God and no hills from
whence help might come. Doctors are worse, for they preach being
patient and letting nature take its course.

Janet's days consist of pushing Hugh in his pram and talking
only to him. The grandiose titles of the housing project, Aragon
Court, and their "maisonette" are as ironic as the fact that there is
no way to get off Janet's "train" (113). She is going nowhere, doing
nothing. Her only resource is to imagine something happening, and
she begins to read about cataclysms and holocausts "to break the
unremitting nothingness of her existence" (111). When the story
of Aunt Con's death erupts, she fears her imagination the cause.

Yet Janet could work for change and get help. The rebuff she
once suffered from the art teacher who decried her work as "tight
and neat and pernickety" (114) is finally no excuse for not trying
again and in other spheres. Her mother wants to help but has been
kept off by Janet since before the marriage, and the daughter perceives Mrs. Ollerenshaw's overtures as though she were the stereo-

typical mother-in-law rather than mother. She and Mark would baby-sit, but Janet does not want them to gain a "moral advantage": "If she were to let either of them make any inroads on her misery, they would destroy her. Her only hope lay in total resistance. They must not be allowed to pity her or help her. She had dedicated her life to resistance, but her resistance must be both total and secret" (106). When Mark urges night classes to prevent her becoming a "cabbage," she will comply to shut him up so long as she does not enjoy herself while she is out. Contradictorily, she would really like to take a cooking class but knows that he would deem it stupid.

Janet hardens her heart against her friends "lest they should discover her secret" (110), her unhappy marriage. When she goes out, she chooses large shops where she will not be recognized and can avoid talking. She has read a newspaper interview of Frances and is put off by her saying that she likes to peel vegetables, one of the few domestic acts that Janet enjoys.

We never doubt the onerousness of Janet's existence but cannot accept it as the basis for her perversity. Seemingly unable or unwilling to confront Mark, she feeds on her resentment privately and looses it on others. She loves Con's cottage for being "fierce and lonely . . . and defiant" (244) while, domestically, she is a coward. She justifies her never attacking Mark on the grounds that she is "terrified of destroying him": "And Mark destroyed was worse than Mark potting shots at her as though she were a duck at a fair" (146). Driven into a frenzy each time she "joints" a chicken (119), she fantasizes about the day when she will stick a knife in her husband. Her alarm at the sound of his arrival or phone call "stiffens" her (134, 276) and frightens the cat; we wonder what the effect is on the baby. At his approach with their guests, "all the certainty drained out of her like water from a cracked cup" (134).

Emma is testily defiant but often humorously so. Janet's spiritually going underground is neither pretty nor safe. She theatricalizes her martyrdom; Mark will "punish" her for enjoying her talk with Ted (139). Moved to tears by an article describing a father's feelings during his daughter's birth, she destroys it to prevent Mark's reading it (149). There is none of the Evans' lusty commitment to battle in this marriage, only Janet's abject fear. While his flaws are reinforced in Frances's description ("horrid little bully" [281]), Mark gets no quarter.

Boredom is supposed to be relieved by dinner parties for Mark's friends, but Janet is not a good cook and cannot abide the conversations. Nothing Mark says pleases her, and she generalizes that he and their guests, not content with carping about local politics, destroy whole cultures and countries in a phrase. The lights go out on their dinner party to sound the death knell for once hospitable England. Here, too, however, Janet must share the blame. The diners are better than she has let them be, and she is the one who would be happy setting tables if there were no guests (132).

Chapter Seven
Middle Age
The Realms of Gold

Drabble was thirty-five when she wrote *The Realms of Gold,* her seventh novel in twelve years; she was still delineating heroines of her approximate age. Set in her own Midlands, the book recalls some of her childhood experiences at her grandmother's (Milton, 53). Its larger theme of oneness with nature was triggered by a television program on the octopus and by one she saw in a Naples museum. The heroine, Frances, derives in part from a "tremendously strong woman" friend who drove Drabble about in a car on holidays (Milton, 51). Drabble herself has no car and cannot drive and deliberately endowed Frances with mechanical prowess. Newspaper accounts of old women starving influenced the death of Aunt Con.[1] As part of her preparation, too, Drabble went on an archaeological expedition and took a correspondence course in geology.

Drabble wanted to give a more hopeful picture of reconciliation with one's origins and especially with one's mother[2] than she had provided for Clara Maugham. She draws deliberate attention to our inability to escape our past by casting Frances as an archaeologist; her lover, Karel Schmidt, as a historian; and her cousin, David Ollerenshaw, as a geologist. The novel is about the obligation to come to terms with one's personal past, with the past of one's family, and with human history. Karel is not only satisfying to Frances as a fellow human and lover but as a symbol of another culture. He and Natasha, Frances's sister-in-law, both Jewish, hold some secret about human acceptance and contentment. Chosen by his mother to escape the Nazi ovens, he appears to Frances to be remarkably guiltless and "undriven," to have none of her restless energy. Natasha (who in actuality is undergoing therapy), similarly, seems at peace with nature and with the disappointments of marriage with alcoholic Hugh. Frances, who is suffering from a mid-life identity crisis, ultimately learns that different people take different ways and that, for her, life will probably never be completely settled in spite

89

of her having moved with Karel into her family's Midlands cottage. She remains unfulfilled in her quests to absolve the Phoenicians of the taint of child sacrifice and prove the underestimation of black culture.

Most of the characters collect artifacts, and Frances keeps her lover's discarded dental bridge in her brassiere. When one of her own teeth is removed, her daughter Daisy embalms it as a souvenir. This penchant for definition and continuity through artifacts is a salient characteristic of Frances, who, in her middle years, wears a string of yellow glass beads she has had since childhood. This novel, as much as any other by Drabble, is about the link between destiny and character: having proven herself worthy by choosing the *yellow* beads so early on, Frances is embraced by fate as a golden girl both physically (79, 174) and spiritually. Fortunately, she has enough charming flaws to make her much more appealing than such an assessment suggests, but Frances "Wingate" is Drabble's "female success story" par excellence. A strong woman who recites poetry in the midst of toothache and childbirth, always makes her mark on hotel rooms, and can wake up at will, she copes by moving into action.

Feminists ought to like *The Realms of Gold,* which was excerpted in *Ms.* (December 1975), but many of them cannot, though Drabble employs role reversal. The protagonist could be "Francis"; her lover, "Carol." Dressed in underpants, she can sit unself-consciously in a tent in the Sahara and play poker with her male colleagues; Karel is very modest. She is a woman of enormous imagination and will: she imagines the buried city of "Tizouk" and gets it unearthed. Like many Drabble heroines, she loves trains; like Emma, she prefers hors d'oeuvres to a meal. Frances also has luck; in short, she is the ultimate "role-model": the career woman with four untroubled and untroubling children.

Initially, Frances appears feminist material—the sexual victim who has struck back. First seduced by her tutor, she married older and rich Anthony Wingate when she was twenty. After their divorce, she has money and a depository for the children while she pursues her profession; their stepmother is even wonderful with them. In the meantime, Frances continues to sleep with men "on principle" (53). She has never been in love—certainly not with Anthony, for she knew she was making a mistake marrying him— until she meets Karel, the most unlikely choice she could make.

The plot is Frances's breaking off with Karel and ultimately marrying him, but the feminist reason she gives for it is not the only one. While her happiness with him does make her stop working hard professionally, there is more substance to the view that she unwittingly throws him off during one of her habitual, hereditary bouts of despair. Worse, from a feminist perspective, is the fact that she does not enter the "realms of gold" until she marries Karel and settles down with him and their respective children.[3] What Jane of *The Waterfall* finds in James outside of marriage, Frances finds as the wife of Karel, the one man for her.

Like *The Ice Age* and *The Middle Ground,* this book confronts the question of what to do in the "middle years" (4). Here, however, that query at first seems posed only for a woman, Frances, and after motherhood. It fitfully troubles Karel and Natasha, but their inner selves are obscured in the power with which Frances dominates the novel. Brother Hugh has retreated into alcohol yet has enough of Frances's golden luck to cope well in the banking world. Moreover, Frances is too self-centered to afford him more than passing interest and puzzlement, and we accept him accordingly. Stephen begs the question by eschewing the human situation altogether, and it seems equally irrelevant to David. Drabble slyly laughs at this theme by posing in mock-horror fashion the plight of Hugh, a grandfather at forty, and of Lady Ollerenshaw, a great-grandmother at sixty-two. Finally, the question is resolved in terms of Frances, though by an outside observer, Janet, and with Frances a touchstone for us all: "There was Frances at forty, as lively as anything, digging her garden, painting walls, writing articles, riding . . ." (307).

The novel opens with Frances alone in an unnamed city where she is lecturing on her explorations. She watches a male octopus and recalls that the female dies after giving birth and accomplishing her role in life. She is in her mid-thirties, her youngest child is now seven and no longer needs her, and she has already been more successful professionally than most people in a lifetime, but she is still always waiting for something that never happens or is never revealed (5), a sensation that will continue to plague her at the end of the novel.

With Frances, we take stock. Lucky professionally, she seems unsuccessful on the human level, if less so than other members of her family. Now divorced from a man with whom she could not enjoy sex, she has never loved anyone strongly but her children.

Her family is not close, and she has found a rival in her feminist mother, from whom she has kept her "real friends" by feeding her "meaningless people, as one might feed dead rabbits to a snake . . ." (68). From an intellectual family, Lady Ollerenshaw is a famous gynecologist who talks so "sensibly" and "medically" (67) about sex that its pleasure is taken away. Karel's wife, Joy, accuses her of conspiring to sterilize the lower classes. She remains a tease and succumbs to hysterics when the starvation of her husband's Aunt Con causes a scandal.

Frances's father is a moody man who suffers from the family strain of depression and "Midlands sickness." Now a vice-chancellor at a new English university, he has climbed too far from his origins. His own father was a gardener, while he, though he has bequeathed his love for the organic life of the Tockley ditch to Frances, has let himself be immersed in a sterile life in which ducks kill themselves against his plate glass windows.

The family inheritance takes preeminence. Frances's natural, feminine clock, the menstrual cycle, is paralleled by a more insistent eight-days-away-from-home onset of the family disorder that happens "like clockwork" (2). Its symptoms—the air turning into "a kind of blue-gray watery darkness" (5)—are those of Drabble's mother fighting depression. This time, the attack is exacerbated by Frances's recognition that she has been culpable in sending Karel away six months earlier and by another reminder, a toothache, that she is not in accord with nature, that her physical and spiritual well-being are complementary.

The disease afflicting generations of Ollerenshaws is meant also to remind Frances to sort out the past. Thus she has been to this same city as a young girl, with the man she was about to marry, and with Karel. The only savory experience was the third, but here she is again without the person who made it so. The seven-year relationship she has so easily severed reverberates with biblical meaning, particularly when we later learn that she was married to Anthony seven years. With more role reversal, Frances is a modern-day Jacob toiling through her Leah (Anthony) to get to her Rachel (Karel).

At Frances's lecture the next day is David, who has heard of her work. They do not know each other but are destined to meet at another conference, become friends, and join in the task of sorting out their family past as they individually sort out the world's past.

A second person in Frances's audience is Hunter Wisbech, an archaeologist friend of one of her assistants on the Tizouk find. Hunter tells of meeting Karel at the polytechnic where he teaches and reveals that he said he loved her. This "fatal messenger" (33) enables Frances to recast herself as Cleopatra and Karel as Anthony, ironically the name of her former husband, and causes her to send the postcard that will recall him. She will make no more cities; she will make love (36). Drabble's love of coincidence again intervenes, however, to prevent her regaining Karel until she has set herself right with the past and her own identity. A European postal strike delays the delivery of the postcard in a wry play on the classical deus ex machina and its eighteenth-century adaptation in the novel that depends for its unraveling on the arrival of a letter of explanation.

The flash of insight that led Frances to Tizouk made her know Karel as the man for her. When he took her home after she lectured to his students, they were confronted by a domestic crisis that evoked his concern and made her love him instantly. Now she cannot believe she relinquished him merely because he kills her desire to work. She forgets that Karel's wife, Joy, has started a tremendous row in her home, that Karel has been unable to choose between them, and that he is an inefficient man who is bullied and taken advantage of by the masses of the "unlovely" (78) but beats up his wife because she wants him to. He has at least saved Frances from ending up like her mother (69).

Frances seems to have lost both Karel and her luck. After she returns to London, she hears nothing from him and eventually gives up hope, succumbs to flu, loses another tooth, and has a (nonmalignant) lump removed from her breast. Recuperating, she goes to her parents, thus unwittingly starting the process of putting herself right with her family. During a discussion at dinner, she begins to probe the interrelationships of heredity and landscapes and of her family and the Midlands in particular and resolves to return to her grandmother's cottage where she visited as a child: "Maybe the old blackbird would flap off on its dirty old wings if she went to catch it" (85). Drabble herself has made such a pilgrimage and has described other successful journeys in her biography of Arnold Bennett and in *The Middle Ground*.

Having conquered Tizouk, Frances retakes Tockley and relives her childhood visits to her grandparents at Eel Cottage. Its kitchen is "the real thing" (171), the measuring rod applied by two earlier

searchers, Sarah Bennett and Clara Maugham, and used again in
The Realms of Gold for Aunt Con and Natasha (258). Drabble sheathes
the adventure in Wordsworthian images of "glorious infancy" (93),
albeit of a *yellow* puppy in keeping with the aureate imagery of the
novel. Frances remembers her stays there as "like paradise, like the
original garden" (87). Unlike her brother and sister, she was oblivious of Wordsworth's condemnation of "getting and spending"
when she sold her grandparents' produce to the passing trade.

As Frances walks back into this "electrocardiogram of her childhood" and "map of her past" (97), she recalls her grandfather's
saying, "with happy submission," that "one can't just leave a garden" (97). The ditch of frogs and newts that has fascinated Frances
and her zoologist father is still there if covered over with scum,
another metaphor for the passage from childhood to maturity. From
her adult perspective, she realizes that scum was always there—in
the sourness and bitterness of her grandmother and in the shame
she herself came to feel at having to serve the customers.

Frances has two epiphanies (102–5) interweaving imagination
and reality and fusing time and experience as they have been in-
terwoven in her walk about Eel Cottage and fused in the frogs of
the ditch and of her travels with Karel. She sees a "field full of
people," an evocation of *Piers Plowman* as well as of "ancestral memory" and "an image of forced labor, of barrenness, of futility, of
toil, of women and children stooping for survival, harvesting nothing but stones." Were the feminists right to see Drabble condemning the exploitation of women and children?

The answer follows in the second epiphany. Frances stops by the
local museum and reads the label on an eel stang as "an implement
used for turning {rather than "trapping"} eels in ditches." She has
the same vision of "pointless rural toil," but the toilers this time
are old *men*. Meaning escapes her but, as with Emma Evans, the
meaningfulness does not. She links the vision with survival and
Wordsworth: "A man with an eel stang, like Wordsworth's leech
gatherer, stood around portentously in her mind, aimlessly searching
the ditches for eels to turn. He meant something to her, she had
not conjured him from nothing, she had not misread that notice
for nothing. What did he personify, that ancient laborer?" (103).

Frances returns to her hotel room, tries to work, and ends up
tortuously probing why she has become an archaeologist and is
dealing with the Sahara rather than the ditches of England, why

Karel's specialty is the history of eighteenth-century agriculture, and why he is "reclaiming the lost land of the Jew" (103). She juxtaposes the eel man and the poet John Clare, another case of Midlands sickness, but one who, before he went mad, expressed his "great tenderness for the creation" (104), as she has drawn vitality from the frogs in the ditch at Tockley and in the European drainage pipe near which she and Karel have made love in the mud. The dark side of the golden world becomes child sacrifice among the Phoenicians and cannibalism among the civilization one of her fellow archaeologists has been studying. Yet she remains muddled.

In a passage reminiscent of F. Scott Fitzgerald's *The Great Gatsby,* Frances succumbs to despair. Archaeology and history dissolve into fruitless attempts to "prove the possibility of the future through the past. We seek a utopia in the past, a possible if not an ideal society. We seek golden worlds from which we are banished, they recede infinitely, for there never was a golden world, there was never anything but toil and subsistence, cruelty and dullness" (104). Then she checks her despair only to requestion: "what is it for, the past, one's own or the world's. To what end question it so closely." On a personal level, she at least concludes that her family's past has been lived for her.

Frances may question her career but has to pursue it, and she is off to a conference in "Adra," Africa. In this miniature community, anthropologist Emilio Spirelli becomes interested in her and Patsy Cornford is jealous. David's chance comment about the flatness of Tockley brings recognition to the cousins and reprieves Frances from sleeping with Emilio. She feels that fate is once more on her side and determines to write Karel again.

Instead, she is awakened the next morning by telegrams summoning her to England and reporting the illness of her mother, the disappearance of Stephen, and an unidentified family scandal in the press. Constance Ollerenshaw, her father's aunt, has been found dead in her Tockley home, Mays Cottage, of starvation. In her stomach were scraps of the paper and cardboard she ate after a broken leg prevented her from getting sustenance or aid.

In the meantime, the strike over, Karel receives Frances's postcard nine months late, a time span probably humorously and thematically selected by Drabble: Frances is generally past childbearing but still labors to bring her life to fruition. Karel immediately telegrams that he is coming to Adra, but she has already left when he arrives.

Sick from a reaction to a cholera shot, he misses a return flight blown up in route, as Drabble enlists fate yet again. Also typical is the fact that his lie is made truth: he told his polytechnic that he was ill and becomes so.

Accompanied by David, Karel finally arrives at Frances's hotel in Tockley. She comes in with Janet, and the reunion is under way. In the restaurant where they go for dinner, Karel, symbolically, "wins the gate" (and Frances *Wingate*), the jackpot of a slot machine. At least, however, Drabble has the grace to tone down the rose color such that he is too ill to do more than try to hold Frances in bed later that night.

Like Frances and David, Frances and Janet have intersected without recognition—they passed each other in Tockley when Frances went to Eel Cottage. Janet not only completes one end of the marriage continuum, but shows what happens to the family member who does not get away. Frances moved out on the backs of her family. David, in tones again reminiscent of *Jerusalem the Golden,* has struggled out by his "wits and climbed perilously up from the flat land, up the bean stalk of the grammar school, to the golden world above" (241). Janet lacks connections and education. She helps to complete still another continuum. On one end are Frances and David, who have turned the family coin to gold; at the other extreme are Aunt Con, Frances's own grandmother, and those members of the family who have gone beyond their bitterness and stoniness into real madness. Janet falls in the middle, and there is hope for her yet.

Mr. Ollerenshaw, the next of kin, turns the funeral arrangements and business matters over to Frances, who journeys to Mays Cottage and learns Con's story from her "artifacts," old love letters—an illegitimate child by a married sailor, his loss at sea, rebuke by the church, a mental breakdown. When Frances buys the cottage, she finds other relics, buried shoes. Her cottage is "not quite as spectacular a rediscovery and reclamation as Tizouk, but it offer[s] many private satisfactions" (306).

Ironically, the communal spirit blossoms at Con's funeral as each participant is lost in thought. The "community-in-death" theme here is married to that of harmony in and with nature as Con will live in the family annals and as the newts and frogs of the ditches of the world are renewed in their fecundity and in the experiences of people like Mr. Ollerenshaw and Frances and Karel. The "leaf-green" telegrams that brought bad news to Adra also merged nature with the golden realms that can only be imagined; in reality, green and gold must be in balance, a theme symbolized by the hedgehog that calls at Hugh's back door for his nightly milk.

At the funeral luncheon, Karel becomes an honorary family member, and Mr. Ollerenshaw is prompted to request a visit to Eel Cottage. The church, the environs, and the grave itself are so swathed in yellow and gold images that we are dangerously close to taking as Drabble's message that, if the realms of gold exist anywhere, they exist here in death. Karel, Janet, David, Hugh, and Frances are drawn through Con's last rites back into the past that is also present. The scene becomes like that on "a pastoral vase, a Doulton vase" (291), a link with Keats's "Ode on a Grecian Urn" and a reminder that the literary "realms of gold" in "On First Looking into Chapman's Homer," the source of Drabble's title, are also timeless human artifacts. Karel's reverie by the grave continues this point of view: "The eighteenth-century cows munched on, undisturbed, in their golden age, by the still waters, by the bending willows, in the autumn light" (291).

Frances eventually recovers from Stephen's suicide and infanticide and so purges also the ghost of the sister who gassed herself, a suggestion that not dealing with the past is allowing its mistakes to be repeated. More was at stake than the history of the Ollerenshaws. Their family malady, which has issued in embittered personalities, suicide, and murder, is a strain of a larger affliction from which even the world's darlings, represented by Frances, cannot escape. The point is, however, that they must and can *cope*.

In another flurry of coincidence, Joy moves into a lesbian commune, leaving Karel and his children to Frances. Later, they travel literally, as they have traveled figuratively, to the "realms of gold"— the "gold baroque of Prague" (304), a journey in honor of Karel's past. Drabble is still insistent upon nexus and has him lose a tooth there, as Frances lost one in Paris and as his Jewish relatives lost their teeth by forced extraction. His aunt's frustrations with the lights going out during their visit also provide a complement for Janet's dinner party.

David sends as a wedding present "a lump of pale-yellow silica glass" from the desert: "scooped, pitted, smoothly irregular, carved and weathered by the desert wind" (307). Its "pale yellow" rather than burnished gold betokens again the impossibility of perfection but the joys and comforts of coping. The imagery of "weathering" here and, throughout, for Frances, recalls the weathered lion of the yellow brick Alexandra Palace at the end of *The Needle's Eye.* The nexus is complete when Frances's Daisy marries Karel's Bob. Families and cultures have intermingled as a microcosm for the world Drabble wishes. David's glass is also a fitting comment on her novels—"apparently translucent but finally opaque."

David and Karel in *The Realms of Gold.* David also prevents an easy assessment of the feminism in *The Realms of Gold.* Drabble meant to give him equal status with Frances. Instead, in one of her disarming updatings of the technique of directly addressing the reader, she admits that he is too much for her, though she has previously told us to "remember him" (43). With Karel, he moves us to a consideration of *humans* rather than males and females, an aim emphasized in Adra's "amazing figurine" with the "witchy, androgynous, yet friendly look, almost a comic look, as one who appreciates the twists of fate" (229). It makes Frances want to do "real work" (222) and is another apt summary of a Drabble novel.

For all Drabble's washing her hands of David, he is an appealing character. He emphasizes the extended family and one's relationship to the past and is a male counterpart for the golden girl. If Frances convinces us that being an earth mother and loving the organic are salutary, he completes the circle with his mechanistic nature and love of the inorganic: "He had a Geiger counter in his blood, a mechanism that responded to rock, as swallows to the magnetism of the earth. He did not really need a computer: all that the computer would do would be to confirm his own innate response" (42). Again, there is no one right way in the human situation. Both Frances and David are successful; both carry literal and figurative relics.

People tell their secrets to David, not to Frances, whose energy puts them off, and he does not have to respond. He is a listener as well as a nonself-revealing talker, an only child who has not fulfilled the stereotype. On the boat he learns about the hostile brother and sister, Frenchmen this time, who are on their way back to their past, a visit to their dying mother, in a microcosm of several of the novel's major themes.

Before Frances knows he is her cousin, she is shocked that David is able to enliven one of the stiff women at the Adra conference by threatening to throw her into the swimming pool. She is also shocked, though pleased, when he leaps up and dances by himself, an act that Drabble has doubtless taken from his biblical namesake who, in so doing, displeased his wife.

Like other Drabble characters, David likes to suffer and to overcome suffering (219), to alternate lonely expeditions with communal activities, and to solve difficult problems and dilemmas. In contrast to Frances, he has failed in his battle with the extreme heat of the Middle East and has succumbed, momentarily, to the family disorder with a "nervous breakdown." His greatest charm, however, is his ability to surprise Frances the Wonder Woman even after she knows him. She, but not Karel, is unprepared for the beauty of David's apartment.

Karel provides another kind of complementarity for Frances in his weakness, inefficiency, and victimization. We infer that, no matter how successful the woman, she is still victimized by love and cannot escape its pulls or help loving the one it chooses for her. In trying to expose some of the follies of sexual stereotyping by making the male the weaker of the pair and having him feel that his children have outgrown their need for him, Drabble has inadvertently provided her heroine with a mate who is not very suitable. Doubtless, she admires him because he deals daily with the unlovely of the world.

Like Sarah in *A Summer Bird-Cage,* Karel feels that wild animals are ready to pounce on him. With the loss of Frances, they in fact pull him to pieces (182). Their relationship has been at the least, then, symbiotic. Karel is the eternal victim who has made a miraculous escape from the holocaust that engulfed his people. He feels, as a result, that he cannot deny his help to the more normally victimized in daily life and in turn plays out his destiny as their victim. As long as Karel had Frances, he could accept his lot with some grace; but, with her loss, he experiences an increasing hardening of the heart against those who make demands on his time and finds himself thinking they deserve what they have gotten. Her return reverses this bad-temperedness, but we still feel that he ought to live for himself to a greater degree, as we feel that Rose ought to have divorced Christopher and made a life with Simon. There ought to be a middle course between solipsism and self-abnegation. Frances is too close to solipsism; Karel, to self-abnegation.

The novel as novel. *The Realms of Gold* is another novel of character strung from a thin line of plot, Frances's giving up Karel and getting him back. Drabble's "theatrics" of style again intrude and make her seem deliberately precious as, for example, she flaunts "a tactical error" (152), makes David "speak, as it were, for himself" (152), informs the reader that "You will remember (or, in other words, I fear you may have forgotten)" (153), or digresses about "coincidence in fiction" (190) or the "limits" of omniscience (293). We are not surprised by her daring us to "invent a more suitable ending" (306), but we may be tempted to say that no male author would have written that way and to wonder if she does not, by such tactics, put herself at risk after such hard work to make critics forget to talk about her being a "woman" and a "woman's writer."

Drabble has worked harder to weld the novel together by theme and imagery. Behind it is the insistence on setting oneself right with family, past, nature, and humankind and the belief that to do so is to enter the "realms of gold" as much as is possible in this world. The task delineated is for the middle-aged, who have gained enough success at living and being to permit them to think about values and about relations to the world at large.

The greatest triumph of Drabble may be the humor, which so happily keeps this thematically serious work from preachiness and from the single-mindedness of the thesis novel. Examples are the episode of the man seeing Karel's teeth in Frances's brassiere and Joy beating Frances over the head with *The Book of Twentieth Century Verse*. We might well wonder, in fact, if the archness of the authorial intrusions is not a deliberate effort to keep Drabble from taking herself too seriously.

The primary imagery is aureate, but Drabble moves out from it to bind episodes and characters by conscious echoes. Nature's creatures help to link people: the newts and toads, Frances and her father; the octopus, Frances and David; and the frogs, Frances and Karel. Craters and voids reveal different human responses, and the discussion by Frances, Hugh, and Stephen of Empedocles jumping into Etna becomes pivotal. The last eventually jumps as he succumbs to the cosmic trauma Drabble depicts as a persistent, formidable strain loosed in twentieth-century life and the core of Ollerenshaw depression. His wife, Beata, who has anorexia nervosa, is a fellow sufferer but has chosen to turn her face to the wall in an exaggeration of Jane's response to life in *The Waterfall*. David loses his cigarette lighter down a crevice and finds unity in the memory of the event. On his way to Adra, he stares into a volcano and thinks about order, process, and eternity. Janet looks at the crater made by her candle's wax and tries to invent another excuse for not joining her husband in bed. Middle age, heat, teeth, dreams, cities and villages, landscapes, various cottages, and literature (especially Wordsworth and Keats) also link people and cause us to study them because of their variations.

As in other novels, notably *The Needle's Eye,* there is a prominent image chain of stones. Examples are the scene with the women and children Frances sees in the field near Tockley, the stone of despair she carries in her chest (163, 171–72, 174, 228–29), and the even more figurative hardening of the heart suffered by Karel. Drabble also makes the point that we should never waste the opportunity to meet others, for we cannot know when a person will be pivotal in our own lives. Hunter Wisbech links Karel and Frances, then Frances and the Barnards. Such interconnections of theme, imagery, and materials give the book the feel of being tightly controlled.

The Ice Age

A similar control shapes *The Ice Age* (1977), whose epigraphs, from Milton's *Areopagitica* and Wordsworth's poem on Milton, closely fit the content. The first suggests recovery for the characters and England, but the second is not so sanguine, as Wordsworth calls on Milton to lead the renewal. At the end of the novel, no heroic figure is in sight. The protagonist, ordinary if well-meaning Anthony Keating, sits in a prison trying, like Milton, to "justify the ways of God to men," but in isolation and without greatness. England's energies and spirit of independence have passed to the lower classes—to Len and Maureen (discussed in chapter 3). Drabble suggests that the elite have gotten her country nowhere—but neither have those who have imbibed America's entrepreneurial spirit.

If *The Realms of Gold* is about what to do with one's life after success as a parent or in a career, *The Ice Age* is about what to do after success has turned into failure and one is already middle-aged. In it, Drabble declares herself one who writes about universals. As Anthony goes, so go Britain and the world. He copes well in financial crisis, but, when he recovers, feels that "defeat would have been more artistic" and that he has somehow been "obscurely cheated" (235, 236). On the national plane, relief is the discovery of North Sea oil.

Anthony is a "child of the professional middle classes, reared in an anachronism as an anachronism" (25). His father is a churchman and schoolmaster, and he grew up in the shadow of a great cathedral. He took the accustomed road ("all those restricting reassuring wombs" [135]): a good public school, then Oxford, and finally a position with the very respectable British Broadcasting Company, albeit in the area of television production. The thought of going into industry simply never entered his mind or the minds of any members of his class. He has that class's snobbery about earning, though he is constantly rejecting the values of his father and brothers. Perhaps the fall from grace he has suffered at the opening of the novel, however, has been foreshadowed in his "premature" marriage, while still an undergraduate, to a girl with the raffish name of Babs "Cockburn," whose fecundity in producing four children before they divorce is thus fitting. While he has taken the very traditional course of studying history, he has, of (family) necessity had to live by his wits and thus has come to appreciate money. In college, he also played the piano, composed songs, and won favorable mention in a Chicago drama festival, and he continues to draw royalties. Such successes rather than his education at Oxford enable him to get his start in television.

The change in Anthony can also be credited to a mid-life crisis. After seven years at the BBC he becomes bored and restless and moves over to the less staid independent network, where he leaves the "arts" for current affairs. In the meantime, the nation has likewise been feeling growth pains and has experienced the property boom of the sixties. It is undergoing a face-lifting at the hands of such economic "whiz kids" as Wincobank, whose name is as suggestive as "Wingate." When Anthony is editing an interview with Len in 1968, he realizes the man's genius and seeks him out. Profiting from Len's mentoring, he originates a partnership in property development with Giles Peters and Rory Leggett.

Anthony is euphoric about the projects of the triumvirate.[4] An idea man rather than a financial wizard, he becomes the "spotter." His finest achievement is a gas holding tank abandoned by the Gas Board and "radiant with significance": "Up soared the heart like a bird in the chest, up through its light and airy metal shell, to the changing, so much before unnoticed sky" (37). We are onto the danger signals before Drabble tells us that he finds more pride and wonder in the gasometer than ever in the cathedral outside his window; we know from the contrast with the mighty eagle of Milton's vision in the epigraph from *Areopagitica*. Yet Anthony's ingenuousness is as appealing as Len's and Maureen's, and we wish that their spirit could infuse the world of "getting and spending" condemned by Wordsworth and re-create it as palatable.

England is brought low by scandal and the collapse of the property market,[5] and the triumvirate falls with it. When the book opens, Anthony is a classic example of the medieval hero who has suffered a sudden reversal and been pitched from prosperity at the top of fortune's wheel to despair. The portrait is expanded by the Renaissance interplay between microcosm (Anthony) and macrocosm (his world) and the questions of chance and fate. He may be artless, but he is not feckless; the punishments that he (with the other characters) garners make us question the fairness of the world order.[6]

Before the crash, Anthony has used his earnings from London's "dense and lively forest of possibilities" (36) to purchase a Yorkshire estate, High Rook House, now his retreat. The novel opens as he watches a pheasant, a perversion of Milton's eagle, die of a heart attack and fall in his pond. At least Anthony is no "artificial" country-dweller, for the Keating family, like the Ollerenshaws, has originally come from the area. Moreover, like Drabble and Frances, Anthony has fond memories of holidays in the country with his grandparents. We also recall the theme of oneness with nature in *The Realms of Gold.* Anthony is recovering from the heart attack he has suffered, at age thirty-eight, with his reverses. He has been kept alive "artificially" as has this dead bird's species. Like so many Drabble characters, he feels thwarted at the verge: his country estate seemed the Promised Land. Bought at the peak of the market, it is a white elephant and one of the book's many prisons, literal and figurative.

Anthony is caught in "a terrible year, a terrible world" (21). The disorders that pour upon individuals in *The Realms of Gold* spread to the nation in *The Ice Age* like iron filings to a magnet (22). Anthony's own difficulties are intensified by his isolation. His mistress, Alison Murray, is in "Wallacia," a Balkan country behind the Iron Curtain that has imprisoned her older daughter Jane because she was in a car accident that took the lives of two of its citizens. Anthony's first wife is, at thirty-eight, pregnant for the fifth time but by her new husband, a nice, safe civil servant. He scarcely sees or knows his own children.

Anthony's isolation is broken momentarily by the arrival of Peter with his current girlfriend and her old spaniel. When Peter proposes buying out the partnership, Anthony suspects that their fortunes have taken an upward turn and stalls until he can go to nearby Scratby Prison for Len's advice. Len counsels holding out, and Anthony eventually regains enough capital to live comfortably and hang on to High Rook House. Success garners success, and his London house sells as well. As Drabble says, "Success may corrupt, but failure also corrupts" (85), a truism demonstrated with Alison.

Alison's problems remain unresolved: "Alison can neither live nor die. Alison has Molly. Her life is beyond imagining. It will not be imagined. Britain will recover, but not Alison Murray." A beautiful and talented actress, she has left the stage to care for this younger daughter, the victim of cerebral palsy, and to avoid competition with her actor husband, Donnell. In her devotion to Molly, she has largely ignored and lost her feeling for Jane, who, now in her late teens, is sour and difficult. Her relationship with her mother is a reprise of Rosemary's jealousy of her sister Alison's beauty, talent, and luck. More recently, Alison's guilt has been intensified by Rosemary's having to have a breast removed. Additionally, she has to feel that she has sacrificed herself for nothing, since her marriage ends in divorce and Molly, though she needs help, does not necessarily need her mother's help; Alison later accuses Anthony of stealing Molly's affections. Moreover, in Wallacia, instead of helping Jane, who has gone on a hunger strike and been force-fed, Alison confronts her and acknowledges the breach that has existed between them since the birth of Molly.

Until the end of *The Ice Age,* Alison carries much of the "condition-of-England" theme. "A thoroughly English person" (105) with a face "as typically English as the English rose" (43), she sits in her Wallacian hotel and ponders England's loss of face. Her words echo *The Needle's Eye* and *The Realms of Gold* but lack their comfort. England is a "safe, shabby, mangy old lion now," ripe to be persecuted. "Powerless, teased, angry, impotent, the old country muttered and protested and let itself be mocked" (105).

Alison, feeling "caged" in Wallacia, longs for improvement and sees none if the future is in the hands of people like Jane. She broods on the violence that has killed Max with a bomb and taken Kitty's foot and on age and death. She contrasts the dirt and violence of England with the cleanliness and order of Wallacia and almost hates her country, though at the same time she cannot condone communism or a regime too old-fashioned to market Tampax. In her confusion, however, the delicacy of the gold wreath and the beauty of the other golden artifacts in the Wallacian museum stand in opposition to the new "gold rush"—property speculation—in England. She is confused and depressed and so oblivious of the "realms of gold" of the spirit. Like Frances, she was destined to be a "golden girl," only something has gone wrong with her world. An actress, Alison phrases the perverting of her life in terms of Shakespeare's *The Merchant of Venice:* "But she has turned from gold, and chosen the leaden casket" (128).

Alison, learning that Molly has been foisted off on Anthony, has to make a choice. She turns her back on Jane and goes home to wander "into some dangerous territory of the spirit" (210). She is a variation on Frances's claim that a woman can deal with a man or children but not both. Here, a woman can deal with healthy or unhealthy children but not with both. Implicit in Alison's biblical terminology (hardening of the heart and washing her hands of [168–69]) is the desire for retribution that her guilt requires, for, like other Drabble characters, she feels that to imagine is to get: "There is no such thing as an accident" (172). On the other hand, "one must continue to behave as though one believed in the accidental. That shows our greatest faith. Molly's fate is an accident, not a retribution. So I must see it" (173).

Back in England, Alison witnesses an episode that binds her to the novel as a whole and emphasizes coping. When her train gets to Northam (the home of Clara Maugham and Len), she has to wait, so she decides to shop. As she tries to cross the street, she sees an Alsatian moving along despite the fact that one whole side has been ripped away by a car. It may be only going some place to finish its dying, but it gives her the courage to climb over the railings and make the traffic part for her.

Dogs haunt *The Ice Age* much more persistently than the stoat of *The Needle's Eye* (and here [245]) and the hedgehog of *The Realms of Gold.* Anthony suggests the reason when he muses on every Englishman's wanting a piece of ground with a dog to complete the vignette. The one he inadvertently gets symbolizes England. Giles's Pamela leaves her old, dirty, ugly spaniel behind; and Anthony, ever kind, tends it until Alison stumbles over its dead body. Later we learn that Pamela, whose upper-class ways Anthony condemns,

receives another spaniel as an "in" kind of Christmas gift from
someone, but it is dead by Easter (symbolically) because she leaves
it in the car over a weekend. In old, dirty, ugly England, the land
of dogs, only the form, not the spirit of their meaning is left; and
they are dying off or being killed off by human carelessness. The
question of whether they will be resurrected remains moot.

Alison counterpoints this theme when, still in the foreign museum, she contrasts the Wallacians' beautiful, delicate gold objects
with the "lumpish" products of the English "assembled into the
shape of a Scottie dog, a pheasant, a poodle" (126). The English
have frozen nature to man's ends and in forms that delineate their
lack of flexibility. Drabble, as omniscient narrator, takes the same
view as she lays bare the "state of the nation" and claims the book's
title in the "huge icy fist, with large cold fingers," that is "squeezing
and chilling the people of Britain, that great and puissant nation,
slowing down their blood, locking them into immobility, fixing
them in a solid stasis, like fish in a frozen river. . . ." They are
"stuck, congealed, among possessions, in attitudes, in achievements
they had hoped next month to shed, and with which they were now
condemned to live" (72). Neither Alison's nor Drabble's picture of
human stasis is the redeemed vision of Keats's "Ode on a Grecian
Urn" or of Karel's eighteenth-century cows munching along in their
"golden age" near Aunt Con's gravesite in *The Realms of Gold.*

Alison is a "light-weight person" (189) to talk about universals,
and she does not last. When she returns to High Rook House,
Anthony is assisting two workers, who, in another condition-of-
England vignette, know no more than he does about hitching a
tractor to the downed elm, a landmark and home of the rooks. Molly
virtually ignores her, and, hurt, Alison goes into a decline and
becomes almost somnambulant. "Held in some cold grip" (211),
another echo of the title, she cannot respond. She becomes an additional burden for Anthony, who thinks she is going mad as she
babbles about her jealous sister.

Anthony copes better. He struggles before the "maw of debt"
(22), probably an allusion to Milton's figure of Death in *Paradise
Lost;* lives with the restrictions imposed by his heart condition; finds
ways to combat his boredom; and ultimately takes on the task of
justifying what Alison labels "God's inhumanity to man" (121).
Unlike Alison, he never loses his faith in England. He evinces no
terror when the elm tree goes, seeing its fall not as a Miltonic

prognostication of more woe but as positive: "England. It would never shake to the roots, surely. An old tree might crash, but the rest endured" (193).

Neither has Anthony become the splenetic debunker of all that is English as has his former Oxford classmate, Mike Morgan, the Welsh miner's son who, for all his success, cannot forgive himself or the world because he is not a serious Shakespearean actor. When Giles and Anthony go to the theater to see him, the audience is "Britain in the midseventies" (237). Rapidly, the jokes and songs give way to harangue until the theater is emptied of all but Giles's party. Anthony ponders why his fellow Englishmen endure such chastisements and analyzes Morgan's answer: "They are rich bitches who like to be degraded" (241). Later, as they continue their discussion in a pub, Anthony has an epiphany (242–43) that gives the lie to Morgan's degradation of England. It cites not only Milton's "great and puissant nation" but adapts Shakespeare with its "semiprecious stone set in a leaden sea": England is a "land passing through some strange metamorphosis, through the intense creative lethargy of profound self-contemplation, not idle, not defeated, but waiting still, assembling defenses against the noxious oily tides of fatigue and contempt that washed insistently against her shores." Anthony cannot picture the future, but he knows there will be one for the nation if not for himself.

Anthony is a kind man and a good Englishman. If his country's hospitality has come down to his succoring Pamela's old dog, it is renewed when he finds the squatters in his London house. With no anger or condescension, he helps the girl, who is in labor, and gives her money when he sends her off to the hospital. He means to call and inquire about her, but he forgets his good intentions and thus does not learn that she has died and that her child is addicted to heroin. When Tim is ensconced at High Rook House by Donnell to help with Molly, Anthony does not expose his lies or exaggerations but escapes to the pub.

If Anthony was not always faithful to his marriage vows, neither was Babs, whose affairs he accepted on the grounds that she is a "maternally spirited woman who [cannot] resist a vulnerable face" (29) such as his own must once have been, and that she needs affection from everyone. He has assuaged his guilt by continuing to pay the way of her generally "non-self-supporting" lovers. He has also felt obliged to give his other women their dues, though, as they usually worked for the BBC, they could have paid their own way. Clearly, it is not merely sex that has driven him. He is attracted to Alison by the "non-sexual aroma of her unhappiness" and "provoked by her undisguised boredom" (42) at the party where they meet. Likewise, when Maureen stays with him after they visit Len in prison, they comfort each other but do not make love. Neither is willing to betray Len. When he goes to Wallacia to bring Jane home, he thinks of bedding her as the only way he knows of giving comfort to women (292).

Anthony is a good listener and a good talker, the kind of man who builds bridges to people. If the aristocracy and middle class cannot lift the country from its malaise and depression, Anthony, who has nurtured both the arts and current affairs, finds nothing subversive in the proletariat as represented in Len and Maureen and in the world of business into which their energy propels them. When God and the values of his father and of the establishment failed him, Len filled the "vacant space" in his life (31) and introduced him to "the Other England" of "stockbrokers, merchant bankers, town clerks, local councillors, commercial architects, contractors, accountants," once only "fodder for social programs." They do not read novels or arts pages, go to art films, listen to good music, or "discuss the problems of the under-privileged" (39).

Anthony has not embraced the lower classes, only their exceptions in Len and Maureen. Yet he is open to the call of the world as few of Drabble's self-involved characters are. He finds zest in change, "unseemly optimism" (225) in a battle of wits with Giles. The American detective series his mother and brothers watch on television is filled with "implausible antics," "but his own life seemed to him inexpressibly more romantic, more dramatic, than any fiction he had ever observed" (226). Unwittingly justifying Drabble's own brand of realism and the "thriller" tactics of the last part of his story, he admits that he "had never gone much for the theory that good storytellers never have any respect for the truth; on the contrary he tended to think that only the truth could be interesting" (163). Neither is he surprised when Humphrey Clegg of the Foreign Office asks him to become a spy. Like many Drabble characters, he subscribes to the view that we get what we imagine; he desired action.

Anthony's recovery seems almost too easy. He is required only to accept the "quiet life, digging [his] own garden, being pleasant to those that need pleasantness" (194), and his fortunes, except for a bad patch at Christmas when Alison is still crazed and none of his children will visit, turn upward. Financially, he has broken even and is back where he started, only five years older. While he can accept that he is a "new man" (246), he resents having to decide all over again and in middle age what to do with the rest of his life. In fact, relief at his escape from disaster undoes him. He goes on a binge, replacing the "stimulant of acute fear" (255) with cigarettes and alcohol. Alison must pull herself from her own lethargy to deal with his breakdown. She also feels guilty about occasionally preferring Anthony the sinner to the long-suffering saint he had become in succoring Molly and her.

During personal and national peril, Englishmen can be heroic; the real danger is the slack periods, a line of thought Alison pursues in her musings on chance and fate. While she could never have left Anthony when ruin threatened, she can slip off now and avoid marriage. Freedom of choice becomes onerous.

In part 3, Anthony and Alison settle into the world they have imagined for themselves. After two months of drinking, he has sobered up, dissolved his partnership with Giles and Rory, and sold a few songs. At Easter, three of his children come to visit. He and Alison think of getting a dog for Molly, hear the thrush sing, watch the newborn lambs, and wish on the evening star. The snake in the sheep's belly comes, of course; critics have been put off by the spy-novel tactics that follow. Clyde Barstow, the English consul in Wallacia, is assassinated, and that country is in civil turmoil but has agreed to release Jane, who, after over six months in prison, is in poor health. Anthony goes to the rescue but has his papers questioned as he and Jane try to get the last plane out. He sends her along and waits in vain for the man who has taken his passport. Ever the English gentleman, he refuses to eat the apple in the man's desk. On the other hand, in his dash for freedom, he shoots an Alsatian, complementing Alison's vision of the one with the torn side. He has been in prison two years when the novel ends. Before condemning the last pages as a foreshortened John Le Carré thriller, we must remember that Clegg has lent Anthony just such a book and that its plot made no sense to him. Moreover, he has, like Paul on the way to Damascus (288), experienced his moment of revelation before the denouement has unfolded. In Wallacia, where religion is banned, he realizes that he does "not know how man can do without God" (288). The rest of the novel is about his adding faith to that concept as he serves his six-year sentence in a labor colony for anti-Wallacian activities and espionage and writes away on a book justifying the ways of God.

At the end of his second year, he sees a rare bird that cancels the dying pheasant and is the reincarnation of the eagle in the Milton epigraph. It is "a messenger from God, an angel, a promise" (320), but Keating, like his namesake Keats, has always been responsive to birds (e.g., to the one whose liquid song makes him wary of Giles and Rory [118]) and nurses his defective heart as a baby or a bird (14). Anthony is a consistent character, his trueness to himself delineated in the birds that make the book a circle. He rebelled against his origins, but when he returns home for his father's funeral, he is drawn back into the cathedral and to a comparison of old and new architecture ending in a reaffirmation of Shelley's "Ozymandias" that again links him with Frances Wingate. He can name his own parody of religious conversion in his embracing of high finance, and he knows that nothing human lasts. Yet he is a Wordsworthian whose heart will continue to leap up when he beholds nature or possibility. He recognizes that his groundless faith in the future is no more functional than Morgan's spleen and that the new order has failed (282) as surely as the Victorian era admired by Clegg. He has a strong sense of his own shortcomings (283) before being left to self-analysis in prison.

Like the main characters in *The Realms of Gold,* Anthony sorts out his past and England's. Consistent here, too, he has endured the dentist's chair by reciting dates as Frances used poetry to anesthetize toothache and childbirth. She yielded her nature to archaeology; Anthony yields his to history. If he has not made it his career, he has remained true to it. When he first arrives in Wallacia, he rebukes himself as an ignorant fool: "here is history, and I can't understand a word anyone is saying, and my only aim is to get out of it as quickly as possible" (287). As he awaits his fate in the airport, he chides himself for having evaded the confusing history of the Balkans as a schoolboy and at the university.

Perhaps the ambassador is right to be shocked when Anthony asks nothing about the outside world. Anthony has traveled widely and has taken a worldview quite consistently. He is now beyond all that. He has read and pondered Jane's copy of Sophocles and is beyond all that, too. Again, he completes a circle as he takes over Milton's task in *Paradise Lost* if he cannot be the "strong man" of the *Areopagitica*. If it is Alison who articulates the postulates of the human situation, its "spots of sorrow, spots of joy" (269), it is Anthony who, living both, hangs on to the latter when the former predominates.

The Ice Age is not revolutionary Drabble despite her having again used materials (newspaper accounts) that other novelists had not employed. In making the protagonist male, she enlarges the process begun in *The Needle's Eye* and carried out less successfully in *The Realms of Gold*. Moreover, she had "done" male characters quite well elsewhere. She may have meant to prove she was not a woman's writer by speaking of larger issues and using Anthony as her principal spokesman, but she forgot halfway through that he was a male and just wrote.[7] The book has evoked mixed responses from critics and feminists, who, though they have chastised her for its male protagonist,[8] might first have been introduced to it through the excerpt in *Ms.* (1977). With her usual aim at authenticity, she read Oliver Marriott's *The Property Boom* and visited an actual prison before writing of Len's incarceration. She returned to her hometown of Sheffield as well and was delighted with the results of its urban development. She also wanted to treat a topic that was obsessing the world, economic woes.[9] While she was writing the novel, a Lebanese friend visited her but left with the outbreak of civil war at home. Though she made Wallacia Balkan, perhaps modeling it on Albania, she, with her rather phenomenal talents for forecasting, glimpses world involvements that are still unfortunately apt. Finally, she had seen Alison's dog from the top of a bus, and the episode had affected her with "sickening force."[10]

The novel as novel. *The Ice Age* is a social novel and a novel of character. Its great achievement is chronicling and moralizing without preaching. Drabble has applied her interest in the interplay of fate and chance more widely and used journalistic and case history techniques without ceasing to be a novelist. One reason for her success is her accustomed ambiguity. The gloomy will see individuals and the world dominated by random disasters; the optimistic, pattern and process.

The plot is linear. Anthony, along with Britain and Len, has suffered the economic and real-estate crash of the mid-seventies. He regains his financial equilibrium but ends in a foreign prison, as Len has ended in a domestic one, through his entanglement in the problems of Alison. She is imprisoned as the mother of a mentally crippled child, and her children are imprisoned by the situation. We are allowed inside the minds of the main characters (Anthony, Alison, Len, Maureen, and, to a much lesser extent, Kitty, Linton, and Jane) by Drabble's employment of one of her favorite techniques, the interior monologue.

More difficult is the delineation of England, which, in a somewhat heavy-handed fashion, becomes a virtual character. It has imprisoned itself in Victorian optimism and empire building and now in an American style of entrepreneurism, with Americans getting to rent High Rook House at the end. We always have to pause while Drabble makes the leap from microcosm to macrocosm (e.g., 71–75, 188, 202–3), the latter often requiring expansion from the country to the world.

Behind all of the prisons-within-prisons theme is responsibility for the self, as, for example, Anthony's desire to be lord of the manor becomes, with poetic justice, another imprisonment because of his using the new economic order of the day to regain an effete image of his country. In short order, *The Ice Age* begins to take on the ironic resonances of Marc Antony's speech on Caesar in Shakespeare's *Julius Caesar,* as well as that play's theme of "how the mighty are brought low" (complemented by Keating's recollections of Shelley's "Ozymandias"). Despite the hype of the media's casting him as the Scarlet Pimpernel, Anthony is still just a man.

The question of the book's moral ambiguity is especially triggered by two minor characters, Linton Hancox and Humphrey Clegg.[11] The former is included to establish England's decline in yet another area, classical education, and to show the spiritual wreckage that results when one is "gifted in a dying skill" (84). His centrality to the "condition-of-England" topos is demarked by his parodic employment of the book's often transcendent bird imagery: in him "the solitary goose of classical learning flap[s] its scraggy wings and squawks[s]" (244).

Linton contrasts with Ned Buckton, who, far from being an embittered ex–geography teacher, has adapted his motivations for choosing his subject and his love for children in his present position as warden of a youth hostel. Because of its limestone scenery, he prefers this village to the Lake Country. He and Anthony reinstate the hospitality of the old England of pubs and rookeries degraded by Linton's Oxfordshire cottage. Linton reveals the futility of the flight from urbanization because he is a "depressing country-dweller"

(79) and the decay of the family because he and his wife indulge in revengeful affairs.

Abruptly, however, Hancox brings the classical tradition in aid of two modernists, Jane and Anthony, who find sustenance in his translation of Sophocles' *Antigone*[12] as they wait their time out in prison. Jane is altered by her experience in Wallacia and particularly by Anthony's part in it and becomes a nurse. Her willful refusal of food just to see what will happen may have been triggered by the pointlessness of Antigone's sacrifice for a "no-good traitor" (307). Anthony is impressed with the excellence of the translation and cheered to find it Linton's. As a result, he begins to take note of his surroundings and resumes his stance as the English gentleman "prepared to represent Queen and Country with the polite and honorable codes of the English public school" (307). The question remains: are those codes comparable to the "completely meaningless code" for which Antigone died? We get no sense that they are. In fact, we learn that Linton also fits in with Drabble's views on human coping. His introduction has updated the *Antigone* with "some interesting anthropological kinship commentary," with endogamy and exogamy: "even Linton, old world as he was, had become a reluctant structuralist" (307–8).

Clegg seems initially unsavory and stereotypical. He withholds facts and manipulates the innocent and naive, his position of supreme knowledge flaunted by his ability to crack and eat a walnut. He gives Anthony the Le Carré novel and makes him a spy. Because Clegg worships at the shrine of Britain's Victorian greatness, we believe Drabble condemns it as having been gained at the expense of the unfortunate. Anthony interprets its symbols in Clegg's flat as "some kind of trap" (281), and the introspection they force leads him to conclude that, though a student of history, he is nothing but a "weed" on its tide. Clegg has jaundiced Anthony, "imprisoned" his view of history, heretofore his passion and the greatest constant in his life, an imprisonment far worse than the literal one.

Then the reversal comes again. Hospitably, Clegg not only takes Anthony out to eat but invites him home for the night. Once there, he proceeds to talk and talk and talk about his domestic problems, but he cannot disclose the secret that will bind him, as Alison is bound, forever. As a result of the maid who dressed him in women's clothes and painted his face when he was a little boy, he has become a transvestite.[13] His wife has left him because she is afraid of revealing his secret, one that would surely ruin his career or make him the victim of blackmail and so victimize his country. Imprisoned by the secrecy of his profession, he has become the prisoner of another secret.

While ambiguity abounds, there are fewer authorial intrusions. The playfulness that remains, deliberately, provides relief from the gloom that is both reported and conveyed. Generally, third-person narration that passes for interior monologue prevails, and we shift from one character to the next, with occasional switches to omniscient narration as Drabble paints the state of the nation (e.g., 71–75, 202–3). Occasionally, too, the plot must be updated perforce since its advancement through the eyes of various characters is limited at best. For example, Drabble has to tell us that "several things happened during the first week of Molly's stay with Anthony" (152) and then report them. On the other hand, she may choose to advance plot and characterization by relating each character to the same event, as Christmas (206–11). Or, more experimentally, she may again do a roll call of characters, including those who have been dead throughout or who have not appeared at all, and predict futures (265).

In the last few pages, there is a sudden shift from past tense to present and a move from a largely interior monologue to the omniscient author. Then, without warning, Drabble intrudes: "This book too, like Anthony's, could have been about life in that [Wallacian prison] camp. But one cannot enter the camp, with Anthony Keating. It is not for us, it is not, anyway, now, yet, for us. But we must acknowledge, we must pay our respects, within our limitations. Into some of Anthony's experience, we can enter" (320). She talks of "our" ability to appreciate his interest in birds and his request for a book on those of Eastern Europe and describes his seeing the tree creeper. With "There, we leave Anthony," she turns to Alison, who, unlike England, will not recover. The ringing question comes back from us—"Why ever not?" Her smug dismissal of Alison is a weakness.

The Middle Ground

The Middle Ground (1980) again places a woman, Kate Fletcher Armstrong, on center stage. In her early forties, she also undergoes a midlife crisis. Like Frances Wingate, she is another female success story professionally, is wondering what to do with the rest of her life, and feels she has lost her "luck." Though of lower-middle-class origins, she has much in common with self-made Maureen Kirby. Drabble is consciously trying not only to expand her coverage of the British classes, as she was in *The Ice Age,* but to break from her standard mold of intellectual women. Kate has little formal education, though critics often see her as a surrogate for Drabble.

The whole of *The Middle Ground* is so oddly reminiscent of the other books in the Drabble canon that it has an almost summational, valedictory quality.[14] It continues the vein of *The Ice Age* with Tom Rubenstein's remark that "British acting was still the best in the world, one of the last remaining fields in which Britain still reigned supreme" (98). Unlike Anthony, Vicky Stennett does eat the apple—as a way of meeting her Underground guard, a "hopeless case" by her own admission (139). The flight to the provinces is repeated by Evelyn Stennett's sister, who purchases a farm in Pembrokeshire. Evelyn would like to move to the country herself to get "away from all this" and *dig her own garden* (136). With Drabble's customary ambiguity, however, Evelyn's friend Stella points out that the West Midlands are "no longer the Garden of Eden, had they ever been so" (140). The "strange year" (255) reported reminds us of *The Garrick Year;* "roads not taken" (259), of Drabble's justification of literature in general. The octopus, so powerful an analogy in *The Realms of Gold,* reappears when Peter's sending a nasty, anonymous letter to Kate is comparable to "stewing an octopus in its own ink" (258). Other creatures, notably dogs and birds, recur. "Unlovely people" seek Kate out like vultures (87). While she tries to set limits, she "marginally" relents and tries to do something about the dying pigeon reminiscent of the pheasant in *The Ice Age.* She dreams of leaving the goldfish on a hot plate, an image that evokes the short story "A Day in the Life of a Smiling Woman" and the end of *The Millstone.* Another dream, that she is wrapped in "this large shapeless garment, and inside it was dark and safe and comfortable, secret and profound" (209), demands comparison with the images of formlessness and lack of definition associated with women in *A Summer Bird-Cage.*

The women-and-success question looms, and we suspect Drabble of venting frustration at having so often encountered the "feminist-or-no-feminist" critique. She was sympathetic to women's needs and causes long before there were feminist movements; Kate is tired of women and believes she "invented" the woman question in her very successful journalism (4). But practically in the same breath, she realizes she will have to do a corrective piece on the image of women in advertising, and she could be describing Drabble: "She was, unashamedly, a women's writer, but men read her eagerly. She created a place for herself, and set a good price on it" (36).

When Kate's story opens, she is lunching with one of her best friends, Hugo Mainwaring, and beginning to recover from a "bad patch" such as many Drabble characters, particularly the women, suffer. Hers has been brought on not only by boredom with her job and by a sense of enveloping stasis but by the old question of childbearing. In the vein of *The Ice Age, The Middle Ground* pulls in contempotary problems, and one of them is the question of a woman having a child in her "middle years."

A flashback tells us of Kate's past with her parents, tiny Walter and fat, agoraphobic Florrie Fletcher, and her older, fat, and odd brother, Peter, in Romley, East London. Mr. Fletcher, a "working-class intellectual," is fixated on sewage disposal and atheism and proselytizes for both. His wife eventually refuses to go outside at all, and Kate has to take over all of the household duties. She also has to protect Peter from the taunts of their classmates and thus becomes a tough and an outcast.

Kate fails her examination for a place in a grammar school and goes instead to the Girls' Secondary Modern at Romley Fourways where her talents as a humorous storyteller emerge to turn her from outcast to queen of the playground and where, like Clara Maugham, she blossoms physically. In her last year there, she takes up with her first real boyfriend, Danny Blick, who is something of a tough himself. He, in turn, introduces her to the arty, homosexual surroundings of London's East End and of the mysterious Hunt, who teaches her to dress and becomes one of the "moving circle" (275) whose center she forms throughout *The Middle Ground*. She has much in common with two male characters in *The Realms of Gold:* like Karel, she is victimized by people, cannot shake them off, and genuinely feels responsibility for everyone; like David, she is a repository for others' secrets.

When Kate lunches with Hugo, she has been divorced for some years from her husband Stuart, an unsuccessful artist whom she met at Hunt's. With echoes of Clara Maugham and the Denhams, of the fear of human touching in many of her books, and of her own relationship with her husband's family, Drabble tells us that Kate owes the Armstrongs "the ease with which she embraces her own children and colleagues, the liberality of her own endearments: they taught her an emotional style, and she is grateful" (33).

Again in the vein of Maureen, Kate bides her time working for a photographer. Her brother-in-law gets her a job as a secretary for a women's magazine, one of her passions, and she quickly takes over for her alcoholic boss and moves steadily upward through editorial work, to features, to a column in a Sunday paper, and to all the free-lance work she desires. Another Clara Maugham, she learns from everyone.

After Stuart, Kate has an affair with Ted, the husband of her best woman friend, Evelyn Stennett, who is Hugo's cousin. Just when she thought her life conveniently settled, she learns that he has been having another affair with a Cambridge biologist and that she is pregnant; she does not tell Ted. Figuratively torn by the wild animals that pursue many Drabble characters and remembering with other Drabble mothers the thrill of giving birth, she wrestles with the question of whether to have an abortion and decides not to until the discovery that the fetus has spina bifida. If we have read *The Ice Age,* we ponder whether Alison, trapped by Molly's cerebral palsy, is better off than Kate, traumatized by her life-and-death decision. A third case is the plight of Judith, Hugo's ex-wife. Her son David goes to the hospital to have a lump removed from his neck, is given the wrong anesthetic, and suffers permanent brain damage. Unable to accept the accidental, Judith frenziedly tries to pin blame through the courts. In the meantime, her daughter Susanna learns to spend little time at home and becomes a variation on the response of Jane in *The Ice Age. The Middle Ground* is about middle-aged people, but it is as filled with parent-children relationships as any Drabble book but *The Millstone.* The marriage of Judith and Hugo also ends in divorce.

Kate reaches her nadir when an Alsatian wets on her skirt in a hotel. We, remembering the dogs of *The Ice Age,* begin to wonder if Drabble has her own special fixation; they reappear here, too (e.g., 67–68, 170). Recovery is slow. With the loss of Ted, Kate indulges wildly in a year of men. Two new elements at length come into her life to redirect her attention. Work has always been her coping mechanism, and she accepts an invitation to make a television film contrasting the choices made by girls now leaving school, five years

after the Sex Discrimination Act, and those when she and her classmates were at Romley twenty-five years earlier. Kate, too, is thus
taken over by Drabblean fate and made to sort out her past. In so
doing, she will encounter characters from other Drabble novels.
Gabriel Denham, for example, is the producer of her show.

The second change is a visit from an Iraqi student, who is engaged
to Simone (a name used for a character in *A Summer Bird-Cage*), the
daughter of a woman Kate met once in a hospital. He and his
complications for her life enable Drabble to maintain the larger
political canvas established in *The Ice Age*. Since Kate's oldest, Mark,
is away in college, a vestige of the "empty nest syndrome" of the
later novels, Mujid can take over his room. The luncheon with
which the book opened was set up by Kate to solicit Hugo's help
with this guest, but the theater party that follows in the evening
seems to bring more confusion. When Kate finally gets home from
it, she finds a drunk Hunt sleeping on her couch.

The next morning, she leaves for Romley and the trip back into
her past to conclude that she has really not changed very much. She
visits her old school, renews her acquaintance with a book of fairy
stories, and interviews some of her classmates for the film. Hard
work and friends see her through, and the book ends with her
anticipating the future once again.

Using the interior monologue technique of *The Ice Age*, Drabble
intersperses Kate's story with the lives of Evelyn, Hugo, and, briefly,
Ted. Evelyn, more complicated and more sympathetic than Kate,
almost upstages her. A social worker, she becomes entangled in the
domestic woes of Irene Crowther ("born a woman by mistake" [239])
and her Rastafarian and is nearly blinded. Hugo, too, is more
interesting than Kate and reminds us of David in *The Realms of Gold*
as he projects the enigmatic male. He is trying to write a book
about the Middle East or Kate (shades of *The Millstone*) or himself.
Ted gets short and (stereotypic) shrift; he deserves attention. Despite
a reluctance to leave these three minor characters, we nonetheless
are glad that Drabble has returned to a happy ending for this last
book. As happened in *The Realms of Gold*, children from its principal
families begin "going together." The prospects are not limited to
Kate's recovery of her equanimity.

The novel as novel. Drabble, who admits that she writes
quickly and seldom revises, does not, after the first novels, seem to
care very much what her readers think. Her brashness and daring

keep her from being a nineteenth-century novelist all over again. She has shown a developing archness and a refusal to draw conclusions and "sum up." In *The Middle Ground,* she again intrudes, parenthetically, to tell us that Wordsworth has been misquoted, give us Hugo's perspective on Ted, and reveal Mrs. Sondersheim's future.

The first twelve pages dip us back and forth into Kate and Hugo; then we receive the blunt and unyielding notice that "Here is an account of Kate's past history, some if not all of which must have led her to wherever she now is" (13). "Form as meaning?" we ask. Kate's past could be disrupting the narrative and usurping attention to demonstrate that she must set herself right with it before she can be self-integrated. Yet, when we reach "and that is Kate's history, up to date" (78), we have only ourselves to rely on for the interpretation of "wherever she now is."

If summary comes, it is suggestive merely, not substantive; for example, "Pigeons, dogs, dead babies, washed-up babies rotting on the seashore—is there no limit to these claims? No, clearly not" (87); "Danny Blick, Hunt, Stuart, Hugo, Kate, teenage children, Black Ice, the dreadful suitors. Marginal people?" (180); or this as another paragraph—"Shadow husbands, shadow wives, shadow parents" (56). The technique seems to be "List and ye shall find," a version of which Hugo performs as he sits at his typewriter (162–74) telling us what he can, practicing, as we very well know Drabble practices, "The art of selection. The art of omission" (183). Hugo's history, we are deceived into believing, "was intended to provide a change of air, an interlude, a nice dry white perspective, a relief from the grit and traffic" (183). It is not "nice" and "dry" but filled with omissions that must subsequently be taken up by the narrator (174–83).

The technique of listing may not be meant as a deliberate refusal to be accommodating but as the symbol of our modern times. We start with ten pieces of "home stuff" constituting Kate's mail for one day (5–6). We get the list of items in Marylou Scott's house (192) and the list of modern "artifacts" (203). What is left but to catalog the characters (207–9) and to exasperate us by including some (e.g., Gabriel, Phillipa, and Rosamund Stacey) whose full significance will be lost if we have not read the earlier books? More provoking in this author who eschews the experimental is chronology by listing: we "began in October, with Kate and Hugo at lunch";

"During November, the following events took place" (215). The reader wonders what to make of a writer who admits that "one could go on endlessly, and why not, for there seems little point in allowing space to one set of characters rather than another" (185)—and this when she is talking about parent-child relationships, surely one of the main "themes" of the novel. What are we to do with a writer who stops rather than ends and leaves us amused and bewildered by a soap-opera/radio-serial list of questions (276–77) meant to set us up for the next book?

We have difficulty avoiding the conclusion that Drabble has come to rely more and more on parody, even of her own style. Why else Ted's "new apocalyptic vision of the end of the world, of a world united not by brotherhood or multinational combines or oil crises, but by illness" (39)? Why else the sweat shirt with the motto "Solipsists make the best lovers"? Is the "ice age" thawing when Kate becomes friends with two members of a gay rock group called "Black Ice"? Has the Ice Age yielded to the Shit Age, as her scatology suggests? On the other hand, she may agree with Kate that we have "spent enough time looking for patterns and trends" (229). Should we accept Hugo's assessments that "modern life is in some mysterious way too fragmented to be comprehensible" (185) and that there is just "too much data . . . we all know too much, and haven't got the brains to process the info" (186)?

Perhaps Drabble chooses to see all and tell all in her novels and yet tell nothing because, for all of her contemporaneity, she floats atop old themes in old ways (e.g., symbol, epiphany, emblem, microcosmic-macrocosmic analogy, Freudianism). *The Middle Ground* might well be distilled down to "only connect," a theme that has played through the earlier novels, but such distillation ignores the book's verve, knowledge, and power. One can and cannot take Drabble's measure as one can and cannot grapple with Kate and her "pale bright-blue give-away impenetrable eyes" (6) or with the episode of the golden retriever, yet another dog (67–68), who moves briefly into and out of her life carrying some message about her not-to-be-born child. Insofar as we can pin Drabble down in *The Middle Ground,* she uses, albeit ambiguously, three major buttresses for her meditation on or "document" (215) of human connection: the putting right of the past, of one's relationship to one's children, and of social responsibilities to one's "extended family."

Putting right the past. Hugo sees the modern consciousness so burdened with the past that it is paralyzed (185–86); and, since Drabble's characters are often seeking to escape their pasts, we are apt to rejoice too quickly at having found the key to meaning. On one level, the "middle ground" of the title is the time between one's past and one's future, but it is also a reference to "the peaceful middle years" (57), an epithet surely denied by the last three novels; to the period when one suffers, like the title character of Milton's *Samson Agonistes*, "gangrene of the spirit" (110); to women at the crossroads of the feminist movement; to the period when one becomes, like Kate at forty, a member of the "new aged" (80); and to the uncertain time when one is free neither of one's children nor of one's parents (185). The time for children is over (257), but Kate gets pregnant and suffers a demi-breakdown when she has to have an abortion. Moreover, to her statement that "the past is the past," Hugo, who most often seems to be Drabble's spokesman, rejoinders, "if only it were" (257).

Before Kate can cope in her "middle ground," she has to get a perspective on her past, a feat that she manages to a degree, though it is we who must take the final quantum leap to meaning. Our first clue occurs early when Kate suggests that she now feels about her former cause, women, as her father (for whom she has always felt contempt), feels about the unions (8). Yet at the same time she swears that her "dab hand" (16) with home plumbing owes nothing to him, the all-time champion of the British sewage system. Nonetheless, the book's virtual leitmotiv of sewage and scatology confirms the tie between father and daughter, past and present.

Having first learned to "turn shit into gold" (23) at school with funny stories of her horrible family, Kate becomes a journalist whose principal technique is to point out the humor of events and make them into good stories. This coping mechanism never leaves her, not even when she is a woman worrying about adultery with her friend's husband and accompanying Hugo to the Artificial Limb and Appliance Center; she gets excellent "material" from both episodes. Hugo tells us in the first paragraph that "many things" Kate does are "little performances" as if she were conscious of preparing to write them up. Driven in despite of herself to share her father's love of sewers, she has passed much of her childhood surreptitiously sniffing at the grate on the Romley ridge, which is still there for her when she returns to her old school (the smell of whose stockroom reminds her of the sewage bank [156]) and old neighborhood to do research on "Women at the Crossroads." Prior to that trip, she has been in the London sewers and appreciates the irony of the sewer worker's putting sewer rats through the letter-box of his ex-mistress (136).

On one level, Kate, like Clara Maugham, recognizes her ties to the past and the fact that she is her father's daughter (120), but she feels, with that recognition, only defeat: "Why ever did she go on so resolutely being what she was? What failure of imagination kept her within her narrow limits?" (114). Earlier, she had "felt that she could bounce out of the confines of her own past like a rubber ball full of spring" (22), but the "passage" into her middle years has demanded a reassessing. She has not been able to disencumber herself of the emotional load of her parents, her brother, her ex-husband Stuart (for whom, though she cannot admit her guilt, she feels responsible [179]), or her interminable acquaintances.

In the course of the novel, Kate "comes right" with her parents and brother by inviting them to her home for Christmas rather than participating in another of her father's rigid meals (123), which she has always hated but has not been able to act to change, an example of the paralysis induced by one's past. Her rapprochement with Peter is shown, as is frequent in Drabble's novels, by their use of the same claim: a person who does not make mistakes makes nothing (97, 126). If Kate cannot avoid her "hard sprightliness" (71) and "maddening flippancy" (191)—again, she might be talking about Drabble—toward Ted, her ex-lover, at least she is aware of them and would like to behave better. So, too, although she knows that she now has the upper hand with Hunt, she acknowledges her debts to him (31), as well as to Stuart's family.

The past, by the proper acts of the imagination, becomes a key for unraveling the present, again without conscious articulation of this fact by a character in *The Middle Ground*. When Kate returns to her school, she finds and borrows *Old Peter's Russian Tales,* a book that has formerly impressed her greatly although she has persisted in denying its efficacy (160) and one whose title may signal the necessity to keep trying to connect and communicate with her brother Peter. Rereading the stories, Kate, despite her insistence that not everything has to mean something (229), begins to apply them to the people and situations she currently knows (162), eventually bringing some kind of vague meaning to the Scott (191–96) and Morton sisters.

On a much higher level, the story of the brother and sister, Vanoushka and Alenoushka, with its "extraordinary" (and Bunyanesque)[15] opening of the pair "setting out to walk through the whole of the wide world," gets at a major Drabble interest and truism— the daring that demarks human action in a world ruled by fate and chance. Such responsiveness is simply expected of the Drabble person: "But where else could one go but through the whole world?" (162). "The Silver Saucer and the Transparent Apple" offers her renewed belief in the "visionary magic of . . . simple gifts" and an opportunity to examine, critically, the past alongside and/or against the present (207–9). As ever in Drabble, the efficaciousness of literature cannot be overstressed.

Similar feats of renewing the present in the past occur with Evelyn's recalling of the luminous lamb (154) and with the memory of Stella's daughter of the apple trees and houses her mother used to draw for her to color (143), a recollection that reconsecrates a flagging familial bond.

In Old Peter's story of the three sisters, "Little Stupid" is resurrected, and the rational Kate knows quite well that such a miracle is not possible in real life (207); like many of Drabble's characters, she is "entranced by the gap between fantasy and reality" (25). Nonetheless, by another act of the imagination, during a moment of total accord with Evelyn, she looks at a beautiful-ugly London "always decaying, yet always renewed." Her pivot is again the old tale as she sees in this London "the little sister" rise up—"resurrected, dug up, dragged from the river, the stone that weighted her dissolve[d]" (243). This image of renewal is grounded also in the Milton epigraph of *The Ice Age* and is repeated in harsher terms here (256); it accentuates Drabble's strange combination of the transcendent and the real. Pulled into it, too, is the stone imagery that so frequently symbolizes the spiritual malaise of her characters and, by extension, of the London and England with which those characters have such a strong love-hate relationship. The water image is another allusion to Milton—the Sabrina passage near the end of *Comus;* it reminds us of the doubleness of that image throughout *The Waterfall* and anticipates the renewing of a future for Kate ("Something will happen. The water glints in the distance" [277]).

Out of the same momentary communion issues Evelyn's vow, once she is released from the hospital, to go forth into London and see all the sights she has never seen. Just for the present, Kate and Evelyn have the answer: human love is the "middle ground" where all roads meet (244). Such knowledge, given the human situation, cannot be sustained, however; even that "lovely woman" (39, 40), Evelyn, a more acceptable epitome than Kitty in *The Ice Age*, has her own purposes suited in the love affair between her husband and her good friend, though she will not admit that fact (56). Even Evelyn has a bed whose downward sloping on her side reveals her efforts to avoid contact with her husband (214).

Putting right the family.   The search for human love and the visionary magic of simple things starts with the family, and the necessity of setting right family relationships is as close to a "message" as any other theme in *The Middle Ground*. Always a latent concern of Drabble, it has blossomed particularly in *The Realms of Gold* and this last book. Intuitively knowing middle age to be the optimum vantage point and having failed with her parents, Kate seeks self-justification in admiring the relationship between Sam Goldman and his mother (96, 125) and in getting along so well with Mrs. Mainwaring, who has not been a conventional mother, to say the least (e.g., 122). Hugo cares for her and worries about her while at the same time insisting that it is natural and necessary for children to reject their parents (121). Kate's fears of flying and traveling in foreign countries stem from her parents' paranoia and agoraphobia and are more of the paralysis of the past.

Despite all the data indicating that abused children become child abusers, Drabble parents vow to be better than their own parents were. Yet Evelyn is excellent with other children but not with her own son, Sebastian, who eventually is "restored" to good-naturedness (240) by the accident that befalls her. Kate, who knows that she has profited from luck and good timing all her life, pays tribute to the "power" that has watched over her family and "let the children free" (269–70). While she does not escape so entirely as Frances Wingate in this respect, she can turn to her son Mark for advice in her anguish over her pregnancy. Not many of her friends really know her well enough to notice her trauma (11).

The family relationship is symbiotic. During Kate's "middle ground" crisis over her lack of career preparation and her limitations as a writer, her friends are not very sympathetic, for they are also undergoing reappraisals (58–59). She falls back on her family, but it now is another kind of trap. She is its breadwinner and cannot stop work to retool but is oblivious of Evelyn's "mothers can't win" (154). Nor have Kate's children any great need to complain (except about the lack of "sit-down meals"); beyond their ken is the plight of the three-year-old in the day-care center whose mother abuses him because he has forgotten her birthday (148). The outrageousness of this episode can be juxtaposed with Hugo's pronouncement in the face of the difficulties Kate and Gabriel are having with their television program: "it wasn't about women and equal opportunity at all, nor even about sexist conditioning in early childhood" but "about sibling rivalry and sibling conditioning" and the "interesting correlations between the behaviour of children reared in all-male sibling groups and all-female sibling groups . . ." (218). Through the exaggeration glimmers the point that one is both oneself and one's family.

Men and women. More ambivalent is the man-woman relationship. Kate, in her guilt, can never be free of Stuart, but at least she does not have to live with the interpretation put forth by Hugo's psychiatrist that she is a castrating female who remained dangerous until she was herself "castrated" ("fixed" so that she can have no more children). Ted feels betrayed by all women and has had one mistress commit suicide. He and Kate have had, however, a symbiotic relationship that has also sustained Evelyn, the woman they have both betrayed.

Most of the subjects Kate interviews for "Women at the Crossroads" have grievances against their husbands, but they will not go public for various reasons (e.g., because they will not be treacherous or because their husbands would help if the wives would take time to show them how to help). One stopped work when she married and had children and is too outdated to reenter her profession, but she will "make damn sure [her daughters] get a fair deal" (204). On the other hand, Irene is a butch trapped by nature in a woman's body, a variation on Karel's wife in *The Realms of Gold*. Linda Rubenstein is "eaten up by a sense of opportunities missed" (99) and makes outrageous statements about her husband. Mad Susan Sondersheim, the wife of a Swedish birth-control expert, babbles about a dead baby in the water at Sierra Leone. One wife gets tired of her psychiatrist husband telling about the man who cut off his wife's head and baked it in the oven and bakes the cat. A mother

comforts the child being berated by her husband with "Don't you
listen to him . . . he's not your father, your father's a vet and lives
in Sevenoaks, so there!" (54). In an example that Drabble may draw
from experience, a female university lecturer who suggests that the
albatross in "The Rime of the Ancient Mariner" is Coleridge's wife
gets silent disbelief from her younger day students and "a ripple of
spontaneous, assenting, utterly comprehending laughter from the
class of adult housewives and retired pensioners whom she taught
in the evenings" (54). Similarly, Kate finds the feminist novelist
who reduces women's lives to "shit and string beans" (58) all wrong,
for baby shit is actually rather nice and bears little relationship to
that male sewer workers must battle on a daily basis. The closest
we come to a stand is the theater party that fails to create "a small
moment of international sympathy." Instead, world leaders and
feminists mingle in the cross-conversations, their only intersection
being their militancy.

Kate takes comfort in being able to show womanly fear during
her descent into the sewers and knows that she has "gotten off" in
her early relationship with her father by girlish giggling and by the
fact of just being a girl. She is checked by Hugo when she asserts
that all of the bad things that have happened to her have happened
because she is a woman (6). Nonetheless, marriage is the root of all
evil (149).

When Kate is trying to recover from Ted and the lost baby, she
indulges in a "year of men" from which she can extricate herself
only by a fit of female hysteria like that employed by Rosamund
Stacey to get to see her daughter in The Millstone. More serious is
the fact that Kate and Hugo "miss out" on each other as Drabble
evokes in their relationship Henry James's "The Beast in the Jungle." At length, she is forced to conclude: "Men and women can
never be close. They can hardly speak to one another in the same
language. But are compelled, forever, to try, and therefore even in
defeat there is not peace" (236). She and Evelyn simply cannot
decide whether life is really very different for men (247–48), but
many of them "have curious expectations of domestic happiness"
(100). Yet there are moments of "spontaneous joy" (182) in the
friendship of Hugo and Kate, though not even Kate knows the truth
about his missing arm. At the last, Kate is ready to go off for a
drink with her (albeit boring) Eurocrat. We infer that, given the
hiatus between men and women, we must simply shrug and move

on to the next encounter. Drabble is not going to take a stand on the woman question, but she gives us a virtual compendium of its issues, both pro and con, in *The Middle Ground*. It is Kate who informs sensible Hugo, in blatantly stereotypical but tongue-in-cheek fashion, that women never send food back in restaurants (3), and what else can we do but enjoy the "pink" birth announcement Kate receives from the American feminist?

As in *The Ice Age*, there is a feeling that freedom is bad for people (7), but Kate's examples are females whose new freedom is responsible for their smoking themselves to death and becoming violent. She also parallels Hugo's losing his arm in Eritrea and her going to pieces over her lost baby. His relief that he no longer has to pretend to be a war correspondent moves us ever closer to the state of androgyny glimpsed here (95) and elsewhere in Drabble, but flies in the face of Kate's summation of herself as mad to argue that the sexes were much the same (7). Does sexist conditioning or nature make women poor at math (20)? Do girls really have a "better chance in an all-girls school" (156)? On that last account, Kate at one point, "but again with a slight sense of treachery," laments that she never learned anything practical, such as *useful* cooking, while a student (203). Kate's forte, as if she had listened to Anthony Keating hold forth about what makes a good story, is to draw her material from real life, which continues to be confusing and to point toward relativity and "situational ethics."

Social communion: the extended family.   Hugo is often but not always right. In the midst of the "classic social horror" (87) of the theater party, he laments to himself "the hopelessness of communication, the bared roots of intransigence" (98) displayed in the competing conversations and, in particular, in the Middle Eastern and Jewish confrontation between Mujid and Tom Rubenstein. But for Drabble, unlike many of today's feminists, social occasions seem to demark the extended family, to be, at their most successful, the stage attendant upon getting oneself in accord with one's family. They also reemphasize the usefulness of the past, for they are the reincarnation of the hospitable spirit of old England.

People do rise to the occasion in Drabble's novels. In *The Middle Ground,* in addition to the theater party (which, in contradistinction to Hugo's pessimism, ends for Kate in the beatitude of Mujid's genuine thanks for the beauty of the evening [103]), there are the dinner party celebrating Ted's return (209–15); the luncheon shared by Kate, Hugo, and Gabriel (219–21); the parties of the past recalled by Kate (262–63); and the party in the offing at the end of the book to celebrate Mark's birthday, Evelyn's homecoming, and Mujid's and Hugo's leave-taking. This last will cross national, class, sexual, age, and other kinds of lines. It will draw in characters from other Drabble novels and will celebrate the communal spirit.

Sometimes these occasions, in and of themselves, may go awry but yield sweet fruit. For example, everyone at Ted's return party, including Isobel, the lecturer in English literature and lover of Wordsworth—there could hardly be a Drabble novel that does not pay homage to Wordsworth—fails to remark the misquoting of that poet. Later, when Ted and Evelyn are in bed, however, the mangled quotation becomes the occasion for a kind of spiritual reunion between husband and wife. Mujid, who has brought self-doubt and a kind of Marxist breakdown to Kate (84, 108), gives her some Arabian slippers as payment for her hospitality. Kate cannot travel to the Middle East because of her own limitations, but, now in possession of this fantasy item, she may not need to. Acts of the imagination, along with ties between friends, can transcend literal barriers. Kate's guests thwart such obstructions as race and generation gaps.

The most telling feature of that party, however, is the communal effort required to generate meaning from the bay tree that Kate, on a flower expedition that makes her recognize Mark's manhood, has bought on impulse. As Hunt says, "our common culture [may be] perishing" (273), but so long as we can combine our knowledge and our efforts, we have hope. Some ancient human imprinting has urged her to buy that green tree, and her fellow humans respond to her response.

It is fitting that *The Middle Ground* end with Kate trying to choose what to wear at her party. While all of her choices may be fraught with "minor disadvantages"—for Drabble is never overly sanguine about life's possibilities—Kate still sees choices, and small choices foreshadow larger ones. In the "middle ground," Kate for the first time has no idea of what will happen next (13), so her choices may indeed be small ones. At the last, however, Hugo can point out that "It is time for the next thing, whatever it may be" (257).

In the face of such facts, as Evelyn has discovered, "All we can do is to join the ranks of the caring rather than the uncaring. All we can do in this world is to care for one another, in the society we have" (241). She says this when her own past has caught up with her and she lies in the hospital receiving the great outpouring of concern from those she has previously succored. She has never expected this kind of reaction; "It seemed enough, it seemed a great blessing."

Literature and life. Evelyn is also the character in *The Middle Ground* who takes the Drabble approach to literature, as we have seen with the Wordsworth (mis)quotation at her dinner party. A similar use of the past and of literature occurs in her adaptation of an Emily Dickinson poem, from the volume her sister Isobel has given her, to Hugo's amputated arm. The passage is dense with possible meaning for the whole book as Evelyn ponders the lines, "Better an ignis fatuus / Than no illume at all—" (248–51).

Significant, too, is the fact that Evelyn holds in reserve the injunctions of another literary "artifact," a quotation she knows by heart from Meister Eckhart. This is one more example of Drabble's pleasing perverseness, for if Evelyn, who pronounces the theme of the book, goes over to Eckhartianism ("Strip away all creatures and all consolation from all creatures so that nothing can comfort you except God"), then the whole fabric ("only connect") is rent. One more episode like the confused old woman at the bus stop (59–62), which Evelyn, in an evocation of *The Ice Age,* has seen as "sum[ming] up her own darkening mood, and the country's," and she might have crossed over. She does not—the whole Drabble point—and neither did a male, Anthony Keating in *The Ice Age.*

Chapter Eight
Drabble's Reputation

Her earliest novels were popular and critical successes, and *The Millstone* gained Drabble a wider audience and was published in a casebook for English schools and serialized (adapted) in a Swedish women's magazine. *The Waterfall* was serialized on the BBC, and *The Needle's Eye* not only brought a BBC documentary on her life but was a publishing event in America. She appears on British television and has had an entire program of "One Pair of Eyes" devoted to her and been published in Penguin paperbacks and reprinted in America. Who else is a novelist, a critic, a lecturer, and a contributor to the woman's page and the high-brow journal simultaneously and yet is so accessible to critics and school children?

By age thirty, Drabble could lead off an article in London's *Sunday Times Magazine* on famous people influenced by teachers. She has been called as an expert witness in an Old Bailey obscenity case, is always being asked to pick the best books of the year (as well as having hers included in others' choices), was one of sixteen academics and authors the *New Statesman* asked whether Britain should remain in the Common Market, has served on national political and art committees, has won three major literary prizes, has been interviewed frequently by American literary journals, and was asked to reedit *The Oxford Companion to English Literature*. Articles about her appear in Italy, Russia, and Japan; and her novels have been translated into many languages, including French, Dutch, Swedish, Russian, Spanish, Japanese, and Hungarian. American doctoral dissertations on her are increasing, and we are hearing of a school of "Drabblerians."

Critical books such as Michael Ratcliffe's *The Novel Today* (1968) and John Fletcher's *Novel and Reader* (1980) comment on her. As early as 1969, she was mentioned in Kenneth Richardson's *Twentieth Century Writing: A Reader's Guide to Contemporary Literature*. Anthony Burgess did not include her in *The Novel Now: A Guide to Contemporary Fiction* in 1967 but listed her as a "traditionalist" when he updated to *A Student's Guide to Contemporary Fiction* in 1971. She is probably happiest to appear in Edmund Crispin's 1977 novel, *The Glimpses of the Moon,* where Oxford's Gervase Fen is writing a book on the modern novel that must include her.

Oddly, Drabble is seen as one of the most traditional of contemporary writers, a virtual reincarnation of the nineteenth-century novelist, and yet one whose plots are negligible. She has fully mastered the modern novel and remained true to the classical literary tradition in which she was educated. None of her peers has demonstrated a wider appreciation of literature. She has single-handedly given status to Arnold Bennett, has done much to renew our appreciation of Bunyan and Wordsworth, admires such moderns as Angus Wilson and Saul Bellow, and has jolted us with her comments on Jane Austen.

Another seeming contradiction laces the appeal of Drabble to women generally. As a woman novelist, she is a female ideal, but her archetype is usually childless and remote, unlikely to appear on the woman's page or write "washing-machine" fiction, while Drabble has worried about writing short stories for "progressive" women's magazines.[1] The women's liberation movement has embraced her and rebuked her, but its offspring are sure to mention her: from Susan Cornillon's *Images of Women in Fiction* (1972) and Margaret Adams's *Single Blessedness* (1976) to Annis Pratt's *Archetypal Patterns in Women's Fiction* (1982) and Carol Gilligan's *In a Different Voice: Psychological Theory and Women's Development* (1982). Drabble has traveled a long way from being embraced as the champion of motherhood and nappies—though her children were always facts to be dealt with, never characters as such. How any feminist could appreciate *The Waterfall* will remain a mystery, but we can understand Drabble's being the first example in an article on "the language of women."[2] She has steadfastly disavowed any connection with the feminist movement other than a kindred concern for the problems women face; and her latest heroine, Kate, is a professional feminist soured on females, herself included. Yet we cannot forget that Drabble admires such feminist critics as Ellen Moers and Mary Ellmann or that, in summing her "nearest" heroine, George Sand, a precursor of the modern feminist, she sums up herself: "she had such a full life and was so generous and spontaneous and cared nothing about petty things, only about true ones. She never cut herself off. She cared for people. She was inexhaustable [*sic*] . . ." (Milton, 52).

Margaret Drabble is a woman and a novelist. She meant to be more than a "woman novelist," and she is. Now heralded as the chronicler of contemporary Britain, she has, from the first, written about more than women and women's matters. She is a novelist of manners as well as of character (male and female), and her surface "trendiness" services a serious and laudable purpose. As another admirable novelist, Joyce Carol Oates, has said, we must read her to know what London and England are like.[3] She reached that level from a progressive concentration on the personal, the family, and the greater.

Margaret Drabble is a remarkable *person*. She juggles, personally and professionally, luck, fate, moral earnestness, persistence, and success. Her novels are richly funny, too, but the characters remain oblivious of the fun, which goes against their near-obsession with the difficult. Her humor is probably a way of making palatable her very old-fashioned "social conscience." It can issue in near self-parody and does so at least as early as the " 'short' story," "Les Liaisons Dangereuses," a spoof on modern love mores appearing in *Punch* in 1964, and as recently as *The Middle Ground*.[4] Her personal success is to have found a balance between simpering silliness and unforgiving and unforgivable self-seriousness. The acceptance of this large continuum accounts for the aim, throughout her canon, to bring the characters to a determination not to live at the extremes. That determination in her own life can be exemplified in her appreciation of both Virginia Woolf and Arnold Bennett, who were certainly opposites and were conscious of being so.

Drabble is equally determined not to make life and fiction opposites and probes their relation throughout the novels. In practical terms, what she thinks, reads, or learns about becomes the stuff of fiction in a special way. Conversely, what went into a novel may subsequently issue in a different narrative mode. The result is that her best commentary on the novels is often not in the interviews but in her journalism. The piece on her last week at Cambridge is the genesis of *A Summer Bird-Cage*.[5] "A Touch of the Boasts"[6] illuminates that book's theme of having one's cake and eating it too and *The Garrick Year's* seminal episode of the woman whom Rosamund meets in the hospital. Emma's reassessment of Wordsworth and acceptance of David Hume in *The Garrick Year* become expanded as articles for the *Times* and the *Guardian*,[7] respectively. Drabble's fascination with trains and traveling produces the first part of "A

Voyage to Cythera" and then "A Shocking Report."[8] She has always shared Angus Wilson's conviction that "the literary imagination nourishes itself in the real world of events, as well as in the world of fiction."[9]

Notes and References

Chapter One

1. Terry Coleman, "A Biographer Waylaid by Novels," *Guardian,* 15 April 1972, 23. I am indebted to Drabble's interviews, cited in the text in parentheses: Joanne V. Creighton, "An Interview with Margaret Drabble," in *Margaret Drabble: Golden Realms,* ed. Dorey Schmidt (Edinburg, Tex., 1982), 18–31; Diana Cooper-Clark, "Margaret Drabble: Cautious Feminist," *Atlantic Monthly,* November 1980, 69–75; Peter Firchow, "Margaret Drabble," in *The Writer's Place* (Minneapolis, 1974), 102–21; Nancy S. Hardin, "An Interview with Margaret Drabble," *Contemporary Literature* 14 (1973):273–95; Joseph McCulloch, "Dialogue with Margaret Drabble," *Under Bow Bells: Dialogues with Joseph McCulloch* (London, 1974), 125–32; Barbara Milton, "Margaret Drabble: The Art of Fiction LXX," *Paris Review* 74 (1978):40–65; "Margaret Drabble in Conversation with Valerie Grosvenor Myer," (British Council Literature Study Aids, 1977)—recorded interview (cited as "Myer"); Nancy Poland, "Margaret Drabble: 'There Must Be a Lot of People Like Me,' " *Midwest Quarterly* 16 (1975):255–67; Dee Preussner, "Talking with Margaret Drabble," *Modern Fiction Studies* 25 (1979–80):563–77; and Iris Rozencwajg, "Interview with Margaret Drabble," *Women's Studies* 6 (1979):335–47.

2. For Drabble's relation to literature, see Jane Campbell, "Margaret Drabble and the Search for Analogy," in *The Practical Vision,* ed. Campbell and James Doyle (Waterloo, 1978), 133–50.

3. See Drabble's address to the Brontë Society, "The Writer as Recluse: The Theme of Solitude in the Works of the Brontës," *Brontë Society Transactions* 16 (1974):259–69.

4. "Jane Fonda: Her Own Woman at Last?" *Ms.,* October 1977, 51–53, 88–89.

5. Bernard Bergonzi, *The Situation of the Novel* (London, 1970), 65; from a BBC recording (1967), "Novelists of the Sixties."

6. Rosalind Miles, *The Fiction of Sex* (London, 1974), 156.

7. As critics have noticed, the females tend to age with Drabble. She cites an exception in *Jerusalem the Golden,* but agrees "on the whole" (Firchow, "Margaret Drabble," 118–19).

8. *A Writer's Britain: Landscape in Literature* (New York, 1979), 7. Subsequent references are to this edition. For Drabble's novels, the following editions are used: *A Summer Bird-Cage* (New York, 1971); *The Garrick Year* (New York, 1977); *The Millstone,* ed. Michael Marland (London, 1970); *Jerusalem the Golden* (New York, 1971); *The Waterfall*

(New York, 1977); *The Needle's Eye* (New York, n.d.); *The Realms of Gold* (New York, 1975); *The Ice Age* (New York, n.d.); *The Middle Ground* (New York, 1980).

Chapter Two

1. Miles, *Fiction of Sex,* 168.
2. There are numerous links. Sarah takes *Paradise Lost* to a party; Clara, Baudelaire to Montmartre, and there is much probing of the relation between literature and life. Names are reused (e.g., Martin, Hesther), and Maugham also has literary associations. Cf. Clara (104) and Sarah on what she will become. Clara sounds like Sarah when her teaching degree is "useful" and "kills time" and when she realizes her beauty. They both have a string of men. Incest is mentioned in both, and Sarah also believes that blood is thicker than water and that she cannot escape her family.
3. In *Arnold Bennett: A Biography* (London, 1974), 5, 47–48, Drabble's reconciliation with her birthplace parallels Bennett's. She based *Jerusalem the Golden* on childhood memories of Sheffield, and it is "almost as much an appreciation of Bennett" as her biography.

Chapter Three

1. See Eleanor Wikborg, "A Comparison of Margaret Drabble's *The Millstone* with Its *Vecko-Revyn* Adaptation, 'Barnet Du Gav Mig,' " *Moderna Språk* 65 (1971):305–11.
2. Colin Butler, "Margaret Drabble: *The Millstone* and *Wordsworth*," *English Studies* 59 (1978):353–60.
3. See Firchow, "Rosamund's Complaint: Margaret Drabble's *The Millstone* (1966)," in *Old Lines, New Forces,* ed. Robert K. Morris (Rutherford, N.J., 1976), 107, and Myer, *Margaret Drabble: Puritanism and Permissiveness* (New York, 1974), 152.
4. "A Success Story," *Ms.* 3 (1974):52.
5. "A Day in the Life of a Smiling Woman," *Cosmopolitan,* August 1973, 90–110. References are to the revised version in *The Looking Glass: Twenty-One Modern Short Stories by Women,* ed. Nancy Dean and Myra Stark (New York, 1977).

Chapter Four

1. The "experimental" narrative technique "just happened" when Drabble was stymied after the first part (Hardin, 293). There are 33 sections: 20 in first, 11 in third, and 2 mixing first and third person. It opens with first and switches immediately to third; the last part is in first. Most critics consider the first realistic; the third, "romantic."
2. Drabble's technique is like the "Paracelsian overplus" of alchemy. Jane has always trembled from apprehension. In the accident, her trem-

bling is violently exaggerated. Then the "overplus" of trembling wears itself out, and she begins to act. Attracted to fast cars (stereotypically masculine), she faces their danger in the accident and is later able to overcome her feminine lack of mechanical aptitude and put together a model of a Ferrari without fear of inducing in Laurie James's fixation on cars. Among the alchemical associations are the images of rebirth and stones, the heat, and the phoenix.

3. Drabble went to see Goredale Scar when she had nearly finished *The Waterfall* and took along a friend with a bad leg (Hardin, 291).

4. Cf. her fascination with the race track music, which she relates to Shakespeare and death (73). She insists her interest is in Malcolm's words, not his music, but finds her father-in-law wrong when he toasts her as the words and verse and Malcolm as the tune and refrain. When she and James hear Malcolm singing of weeping and fountains (77), images of her relation with James, she does not see that her husband is more suited to her. When she looks for foreshadowings, she ignores the fact that she and Malcolm hit the post in the water with stones while James missed. She pretends to be passive but imposes interpretations that suit her.

5. She also alludes to the board of the Quakers. Her application of religious terms to secular love draws on Romeo and Juliet's exchange on love's "pilgrimage" and has been noticed by Joan S. Korenman, "The 'Liberation' of Margaret Drabble," *Critique* 21 (1980):62, and Roberta Rubenstein, "*The Waterfall:* The Myth of Psyche, Romantic Tradition, and the Female Quest," in *Margaret Drabble,* ed. Schmidt, 139–57.

6. Drabble took these changes, used again in *The Realms of Gold,* from the symptoms of her mother during bouts of depression.

7. Interestingly, Jane, who is by name (despite the spelling difference) linked with the historical Jane Grey and thus with a king, Edward VI, is associated with two men with kingly names. She aligns herself with Lady Macbeth (137), and "Malcolm" becomes the true king at the end of Shakespeare's *Macbeth* and must be "wooed" back to England.

8. "The Reunion," in *Winter's Tales 14,* ed. Kevin Crossley-Holland (London, 1968), 168; references are to this version. A shorter version, under the title "Faithful Lovers," appeared in the *Saturday Evening Post,* 6 April 1968, 62, 64–65.

9. "A Voyage to Cythera," *Mademoiselle,* December 1967, 99.

10. Ellen Cronan Rose, "Margaret Drabble: Surviving the Future," *Critique* 15 (1973):8, and Suzanne H. Mayer, "Margaret Drabble's Short Stories: Worksheets for her Novels," in *Margaret Drabble,* ed. Schmidt, 80, relate "A Voyage to Cythera" to *Jerusalem the Golden.* An additional reason for my connecting it with *The Waterfall* is their taking off from paintings: Antoine Watteau's "The Pilgrimage to Cythera" (or the "em-

barcation for Cythera" tradition generally) and James Ward's "Goredale Scar: Yorkshire," respectively. Drabble is very interested in art (e.g., the artists in "A Success Story," Salvator Rosa's "Empedocles" in *The Realms of Gold*, "Psyche Locked Out of the Palace of Cupid" in *The Middle Ground*).

Chapter Five

1. Drabble, in "The Author Comments," *Dutch Quarterly Review of Anglo-American Letters* 5 (1975):35, says the ending is seen by "women in particular, and Women's Liberation even more particularly" as "some kind of sell-out." She might have changed it if she and her husband had already been separated (Hardin, 277).

2. Mel Gussow, "Margaret Drabble: A Double Life," *New York Times Book Review*, 9 October 1977, 40.

3. See "In View of the Poor," *Times Literary Supplement*, 31 March 1972, 353.

4. "The Author Comments," 35.

5. Ibid., 36.

6. See Lynn Veach Sadler, *John Bunyan* (Boston: Twayne, 1979), 38.

7. "The Author Comments," 38.

8. *Arnold Bennett*, 294.

9. "The Gifts of War," *Winter's Tales 16,* ed. A. D. Maclean (London, 1970), 35.

10. "Homework," *Ontario Review*, Fall–Winter 1977–78, 9.

11. "Hassan's Tower," in *Winter's Tales 12,* ed. A. D. Maclean (London, 1966), 45.

12. "Crossing the Alps," *Mademoiselle,* February 1971, 155.

Chapter Six

1. Drabble reports the biographical links in the Hardin interview (291). She remembers her stuttering in Mike Papini.

2. Jonathan Raban, *The Technique of Modern Fiction* (London, 1968), 93.

3. For example, François Bonfond, "Margaret Drabble: How to Express Subjective Truth Through Fiction?," *Revue des langues vivantes* 40 (1974):48; Cynthia L. Brown and Karen Olson, eds., *Feminist Criticism: Essays on Theory, Poetry and Prose* (Metuchen, N.J., and London: Scarecrow Press, 1978), 286; Judith Ruderman, "An Invitation to a Dinner Party: Margaret Drabble on Women and Food," in *Margaret Drabble,* ed. Schmidt, 104–16; Irving Wardle, "How to Catch the Reader's Attention," *Observer,* 19 July 1964, 23.

Chapter Seven

1. Gussow, "Margaret Drabble," 40.

2. Rose, in chapter 5 of *The Novels of Margaret Drabble* (Totowa, N.J., 1980), 94–111, discusses matrophobia and a kinship network traced through mothers.

3. Drabble "was perfectly aware that [her] feminist critics weren't going to like [her] ending the book with a marriage" (Cooper-Clark, 75).

4. Like Frances Wingate, Anthony draws on Shakespeare's *Antony and Cleopatra*. Frances imagines Karel and herself the famous lovers. Anthony parallels Giles, Rory and himself with Shakespeare's Caesar, Lepidus, and Antony.

5. For the troubles and scandals alluded to in *The Ice Age,* see Adele Freedman, "No More Happy Endings?" *Canadian Forum* 57 (1977–78):40, and Paul Bailey, "Of Prophecy and Puppetry," *Saturday Review* 5 (1978):39–40.

6. Anthony reads Boethius's *Consolation of Philosophy* in prison, and Edith Milton, "Books Considered—*The Ice Age* by Margaret Drabble," *New Republic* 177 (1977):28–30, makes it as integral to the novel as I have Bunyan to *The Needle's Eye.*

7. Ralph Tyler, "*Bookviews* Talks to Edna O'Brien and Margaret Drabble," *Bookviews* 1 (1978):7.

8. Cf. Maureen and Alison "amused" by their "female attitude that men are children who need to be kept busy, to keep them out of mischief" (260) and Anthony finding (289) women better at languages.

9. For the novel's genesis, see Gussow, "Margaret Drabble," and the Milton interview.

10. Margaret Forster, "What Makes Margaret Drabble Run and Run," *Guardian,* 28 February 1981, 9.

11. Drabble is also ambiguous about the relation of the one and the many, the theme prominent in *The Realms of Gold* and in the microcosmic-macrocosmic linkage here. Alison sees both sides (178); cf. Anthony, 237.

12. For an extended discussion of the influence of the *Antigone,* see Gerhard Joseph, "The *Antigone* as Cultural Touchstone: Matthew Arnold, Hegel, George Eliot, Virginia Woolf, and Margaret Drabble," *PMLA* 96 (1981):22–35.

13. In *The Waterfall,* James's mother dresses him in her clothes.

14. In a letter to the author (14 September 1983), Drabble does not know what she will do after reediting *The Oxford Companion to English Literature,* but she hopes to do "something entirely different."

15. See 138, 171–72 for Bunyanesque images.

Chapter Eight

1. "Langham Diary," *Listener,* 7 February 1974, 164.

2. Virginia Tiger and Gina Luria, "Inlaws/Outlaws: The Language of Women," in *Women's Language and Style,* ed. Douglas Butturff and Edmund I. Epstein, Studies in Contemporary Language, no. 1 (Akron: University of Akron, 1978), 1.

3. Joyce Carol Oates, "Bricks and Mortar," *Ms.,* August 1974, 35.

4. Not enough is made of Drabble's tongue-in-cheek writing, for example, "My Next Husband," *Punch,* 1 September 1965, 310–12, and "Baffled! Margaret Drabble Stalks Uncomprehendingly Round the Mystery of Masculinity," *Punch,* 24 July 1968, 122–24.

5. "The Month," *Twentieth Century,* July 1960, 73–78.

6. "A Touch of the Boasts," *Punch,* 9 February 1966, 188–89.

7. "So Honourably Born," *London Times,* 14 December 1968, 17, and "The Sexual Revolution," *Guardian,* 11 October 1967, 8.

8. "A Shocking Report," *Author* 80 (1969):169–71.

9. " 'No Idle Rentier': Angus Wilson and the Nourished Literary Imagination," *Studies in the Literary Imagination* 13 (1980):129.

Selected Bibliography

PRIMARY SOURCES

1. Novels (listed chronologically)

A Summer Bird-Cage. London: Weidenfeld & Nicolson, 1963; New York: Morrow, 1964; Harmondsworth: Penguin, 1967; New York: Belmont, 1971.

The Garrick Year. London: Weidenfeld & Nicolson, 1964; New York: Morrow, 1965; Harmondsworth: Penguin, 1966; New York: Popular Library, 1977.

The Millstone. London: Weidenfeld & Nicolson, 1965; New York: Morrow, 1966; Harmondsworth: Penguin, 1968. Reprint. *Thank You All Very Much.* New York: New American Library, 1969. Reprinted as casebook with introduction by Drabble: London: Longman, 1970.

Jerusalem the Golden. London: Weidenfeld & Nicolson, 1967; New York: Morrow, 1967; Harmondsworth: Penguin, 1969; New York: Belmont, 1971.

The Waterfall. London: Weidenfeld & Nicolson, 1969; Harmondsworth: Penguin, 1971; New York: Knopf, 1969; New York: Fawcett, 1977.

The Needle's Eye. London: Weidenfeld & Nicolson, 1972; New York: Knopf, 1972; Harmondsworth: Penguin, 1973; New York: Popular Library, n.d.

The Realms of Gold. London: Weidenfeld & Nicolson, 1975; New York: Knopf, 1975; New York: Popular Library, n.d.

The Ice Age. London: Weidenfeld & Nicolson, 1977; New York: Knopf, 1977.

The Middle Ground. London: Weidenfeld & Nicolson, 1980; New York: Knopf, 1980.

2. Short stories (listed chronologically)

" 'Les Liaisons Dangereuses': Margaret Drabble on the Strategy of Modern Love." *Punch,* 28 October 1964, 646–48.

"Hassan's Tower." In *Winter's Tales 12,* edited by A. D. Maclean, 41–59. London: Macmillan, 1966.

"A Voyage to Cythera." *Mademoiselle,* December 1967, 98–99, 148–50.

"The Reunion." In *Winter's Tales 14,* edited by Kevin Crossley-Holland, 149–68. London: Macmillan, 1968.

"A Pyrrhic Victory." *Nova*, July 1968, 80, 84, 86; *Saturday Evening Post*, 6 April 1968, 62, 64–65.

"Crossing the Alps." In *Penguin Modern Stories 3*, edited by Judith Burnley, 63–85. Harmondsworth: Penguin, 1969. Reprint. *Mademoiselle*, February 1971, 154–55, 193–98.

"The Gifts of War." In *Winter's Tales 16*, edited by A. D. Maclean, 20–36. London: Macmillan, 1970. Reprint. In *Women and Fiction: Short Stories by and about Women*, edited by Susan Cahill, 335–47. New York: New American Library, 1975.

"A Success Story." *Spare Rib*, no. 2 (1972):26–27, 33. Reprinted in *Ms.*, December 1974, 52, 54–55, 94.

"A Day in the Life of a Smiling Woman." *Cosmopolitan*, August 1973, 90–110. Reprinted in *The Looking Glass: Twenty-One Modern Short Stories by Women*, edited by Nancy Dean and Myra Stark, 143–65. New York: Putnam, 1977.

"Homework." *Ontario Review*, Fall–Winter 1977–78, 7–13.

3. Nonfiction (listed chronologically)

Wordsworth. Literature in Perspective. London: Evans Brothers, 1966; New York: Arco, 1969.

London Consequences. London: Greater London Arts Association, 1972. Coeditor with B. S. Johnson.

Virginia Woolf: A Personal Debt. N.p.: Aloe Editions, 1973. Earlier appeared as "How Not to Be Afraid of Virginia Woolf." *Ms.*, November 1972, 68–70, 72, 121.

Arnold Bennett: A Biography. London: Weidenfeld & Nicolson, 1974; New York: Knopf, 1974.

Lady Susan, The Watsons, Sanditon, by Jane Austen. Harmondsworth: Penguin, 1974. Edited.

The Genius of Thomas Hardy. London: Weidenfeld & Nicolson, 1976; New York: Knopf, 1976. Edited. See 162–69: "Hardy and the Natural World."

For Queen and Country: Britain in the Victorian Age. Mirror of Britain Series. London: Andre Deutsch, 1978; New York: Seabury, 1979.

A Writer's Britain: Landscape in Literature. New York: Knopf, 1979.

SECONDARY SOURCES

1. Bibliographies

Schmidt, Dorey. "A Bibliography Update (1977–1981)." In *Margaret Drabble: Golden Realms*, edited by Schmidt, 186–93. Living Author

Series, no. 4. Edinburg, Tex.: Pan American University Press, 1982. Updates Stanton and adopts his divisions.

Stanton, Robert J. *A Bibliography of Modern British Novelists.* Troy, N.Y.: Whitston, 1978. 1:181–213; 346 items.

2. Books

Bergonzi, Bernard. *The Situation of the Novel.* London: Macmillan, 1970, 56–79. Includes Drabble's comments on experimentation. Interesting juxtaposition of Drabble and sister, A. S. Byatt.

Campbell, Jane. "Margaret Drabble and the Search for Analogy." In *The Practical Vision: Essays in English Literature in Honour of Flora Roy,* edited by Campbell and James Doyle, 133–50. Waterloo: Wilfrid Laurier University Press, 1978. The most complete account of Drabble's use of literature.

Cunningham, Gail. "Women and Children First: The Novels of Margaret Drabble." In *Twentieth-Century Women Novelists,* edited by Thomas F. Staley, 130–52. Totowa, N.J.: Barnes & Noble, 1982. Traces two thematic foci, literary references and children, in the first eight novels.

Firchow, Peter E. "Rosamund's Complaint: Margaret Drabble's *The Millstone* (1966)." In *Old Lines, New Forces: Essays on the Contemporary British Novel, 1960–1970,* edited by Robert K. Morris, 93–108. London: Associated University Presses, 1976. A close reading. Highlights are the imagery of machinery, relation to Samuel Daniel, and interplay between Bentham and Burke.

———, ed. *The Writer's Place: Interviews on the Literary Situation in Contemporary Britain.* Minneapolis: University of Minnesota Press, 1974, 102–21. Early interview (1969) but still valuable for relation between Drabble biography and writings. Drabble aims to get novels serious.

McCulloch, Joseph. "Dialogue with Margaret Drabble." In *Under Bow Bells: Dialogues with Joseph McCulloch.* London: Sheldon Press, 1974, 125–32. An early interview stressing Drabble's view of the writer.

Moran, Mary Hurley. *Margaret Drabble: Existing within Structures.* Carbondale: Southern Illinois University Press, 1983. Essential. An extended treatment of the characters' will to survive in a world lacking freedom and of the individual's relationship to family, nature, and the imagination. Drabble not just a woman's writer but has larger concerns.

Myer, Valerie Grosvenor. *Margaret Drabble: Puritanism and Permissiveness.* London: Vision, 1974. Emphasizes influence of Drabble's biography, especially Quakerism, on the novels and traces characters' doubts and scruples to Drabble's being crippled by her "puritanism." Good on Drabble as artist.

Rose, Ellen Cronan, ed. *Critical Essays on Margaret Drabble*. Boston: G. K. Hall. 1985.

————. *The Novels of Margaret Drabble: Equivocal Figures*. Totowa, N.J.: Barnes & Noble, 1980. Sees Drabble developing artistic control but remaining ambivalent about feminism.

Schmidt, Dorey, ed. *Margaret Drabble: Golden Realms*. Living Author Series, no. 4. Edinburg, Tex.: Pan American University Press, 1982. Important collection of essays attesting to Drabble's status in America. Most widely applicable: Mayer on the short stories, Ruderman on Drabble's change in attitude toward dinner parties, Levitt on Drabble's Victorianism. Dixson original in symbolism of names in *The Needle's Eye*. Efrig sees *The Middle Ground* moving beyond women's questions. Bromberg on *The Realms of Gold* and Rubenstein on *The Waterfall* particularly interesting.

Seiler-Franklin, Carol. *Boulder-Pushers: Women in the Fiction of Margaret Drabble, Doris Lessing, and Iris Murdoch*. Bern: Peter Lang, 1979. Nonacademic. For "women who want to know their counterparts" and "men who want to know women's problems." Classifies women.

3. Articles

Apter, T. E. "Margaret Drabble: The Glamour of Seriousness." *Human World*, August 1973, 18–28. Negative view of Drabble as a superficial recorder of life.

Beards, Virginia K. "Margaret Drabble: Novels of a Cautious Feminist." *Critique* 15 (1973):35–47. Drabble the total feminist but chooses the role of artist rather than activist. Her novels explore the options of today's women.

Bonfond, François. "Margaret Drabble: How to Express Subjective Truth Through Fiction?" *Revue des langues vivantes* 40 (1974):41–55. The contents of the first four novels are almost exclusively personal. Readers thrilled by recognition of her modern content.

Butler, Colin. "Margaret Drabble: *The Millstone* and Wordsworth." *English Studies* 59 (1978):353–60. Drabble without hope in the Wordsworthian sense and makes Wordsworth too much of a realist. Both books lack a social dimension.

Campbell, Jane. "Becoming Terrestrial: The Short Stories of Margaret Drabble." *Critique* 25 (1983):25–44. The fullest treatment of the short stories. Especially apt on the "indeterminate endings" and the relation to ordinary experience.

————. "Reaching Outwards: Versions of Reality in *The Middle Ground*." *Journal of Narrative Technique* 14 (1984):17–32. A perceptive assessment of the novel's inconclusiveness.

Clare, John. "Margaret Drabble's Everyday Hell." *London Times,* 27 March 1972, 6. A review of *The Needle's Eye* and an interview of Drabble. Most interesting: her cyclic temper, Quaker influence, lodger who baby-sits, and enjoyment of dinner parties.

Coleman, Terry. "A Biographer Waylaid by Novels." *Guardian,* 15 April 1972, 23. An interview: Drabble talks on why there are so many first-rate women novelists and on changes in male-female relations.

Cooper-Clark, Diana. "Margaret Drabble: Cautious Feminist." *Atlantic Monthly,* November 1980, 69–75. An essential interview. Drabble says her books not "about" feminism, just easier to write about her own sex; best novelists androgynous. Her view of literature and many literary figures, including Bunyan, who "profoundly affected her moral thinking." Denies knowing what her images mean.

Davis, Cynthia A. "Unfolding Form: Narrative Approach and Theme in *The Realms of Gold." Modern Language Quarterly* 40 (1979):390–402. Interesting explanation for novels calling attention to themselves as stories: Drabble's use of some of the techniques of "self-reflexive fiction." Much on Victorianism in *The Realms of Gold.*

Edwards, Lee R. "*Jerusalem the Golden:* A Fable for Our Times." *Women's Studies* 6 (1979):321–34. Clara fulfills the course of the typical male comic hero.

Forster, Margaret. "What Makes Margaret Drabble Run and Run." *Guardian,* 28 February 1981, 9. Biographical. Gives good sense of Drabble's current status as writer. Denies being dissatisfied with first five novels. Forster: Drabble has yet to do her best work.

Fox-Genovese, Elizabeth. "The Ambiguities of Female Identity: A Reading of the Novels of Margaret Drabble." *Partisan Review* 46 (1979):234–48. An excellent if negative analysis of Drabble's "divorce between sign and referent," trendiness, failure to come to terms with heroines' denial of other women. Drabble should not waste talent on such heroines.

Gussow, Mel. "Margaret Drabble: A Double Life." *New York Times Book Review,* 9 October 1977, 7, 40–41. Largely biographical. Based on interview. Drabble's double life: novelist and mother/housewife. Drabble traces industriousness from Yorkshire heritage.

Hardin, Nancy S. "Drabble's *The Millstone:* A Fable for Our Times." *Critique* 15 (1973):22–34. Traces Rosamund's growth from naiveté to knowledge as contemporary moral fable. Good discussion of Drabble's use of Daniel's *Complaint* and of other literature.

————. "An Interview with Margaret Drabble." *Contemporary Literature* 14 (1973):273–95. Essential for Drabble biography. Of especial importance, Drabble on her kinship with nineteenth-century novelists, grace, Bunyan, and her heroines. Maintains she is not a feminist. Draws her characters from life—her own and others'.

Horder, John. "Heroine in an Empty House." *London Times,* 21 May 1969, 12. Much on *The Waterfall. The Millstone* brought Drabble a wider reading public. Her lack of assertiveness, nightmares about children, inability to do nothing, worries about causing offense, paralyzing episode in launderette.

Kaplan, Carey. "A Vision of Power in Margaret Drabble's *The Realms of Gold." Journal of Women's Studies in Literature* 1 (1979):233–42. Tantalizing discussion of uterine imagery.

Klein, Norma. "Real Novels about Real Women." *Ms.,* September 1972, 7–8. Summary of Drabble after the first six novels. Originality in self-confidence of heroines. Drabble ironic toward but on their side and their situations applicable to women anywhere.

Korenman, Joan S. "The 'Liberation' of Margaret Drabble." *Critique* 21 (1980):61–72. Earlier novels on problems confronting contemporary women; later, on what happens if equality achieved—still left with question of whether "this is all."

Lambert, Ellen Z. "Margaret Drabble and the Sense of Possibility." *University of Toronto Quarterly* 49 (1980):228–51. Drabble may take life as "possibility" from Arnold Bennett. On *A Summer Bird-Cage, Jerusalem the Golden, The Realms of Gold.* Identifies "the Drabble heroine."

Lay, Mary M. "Temporal Ordering in the Fiction of Margaret Drabble." *Critique* 21 (1980):73–84. On *The Needle's Eye, The Realms of Gold, The Ice Age.* Temporal ordering allows Drabble to highlight the past, isolation, fate, and the environment as themes.

Libby, Marion Vlastos. "Fate and Feminism in the Novels of Margaret Drabble." *Contemporary Literature* 16 (1975):175–92. Drabble focuses on fatalism and will, also feminist concerns. First six novels, except for *Jerusalem the Golden,* show her development as a writer. Her uniqueness is the appreciation of the beauty and value of children. The society she describes is class-bound and patriarchal.

Little, Judy. "Margaret Drabble and the Romantic Imagination: *The Realms of Gold." Prairie Schooner* 55 (1981):241–52. Drabble influenced by Wordsworth for effect of environment and interplay of imagination. Her "golden worlds" recede but not quite.

MacCarthy, Fiona. "The Drabble Sisters." *Guardian,* 13 April 1967, 8. Strict professional secrecy maintained by the three: Susan (A. S. Byatt), scholar/novelist; Margaret; and Helen, the youngest, an art historian. Talk about children when they meet.

Manheimer, Joan. "Margaret Drabble and the Journey to the Self." *Studies in the Literary Imagination* 11 (1978):127–43. Applies Freud. Heroines struggle for identity as society shackles with "inverse doubles." Drabble finds solution in *The Waterfall*.

Mannheimer, Monica Lauritzen. "The Search for Identity in Margaret Drabble's *The Needle's Eye*," *Dutch Quarterly Review of Anglo-American Letters* 5 (1975):24–35. Rose's main motive is mystical need for salvation through sacrifice. A "sad and defeatist novel." Refuted by Drabble.

Milton, Barbara. "Margaret Drabble: The Art of Fiction LXX." *Paris Review*, Fall–Winter 1978, 40–65. Interview. On home, work habits, names, portrayal of mothers, terror of boredom, Freud, coincidence. Most fond of *The Needle's Eye*. Admires Angus Wilson, Bellow, Lessing but does not like placing writers. A novel should explore new territory.

Milton, Edith. "Books Considered—*The Ice Age* by Margaret Drabble." *New Republic*, 22 October 1977, 28–30. Persuasive argument that Drabble consciously using Boethius's *Consolation of Philosophy* throughout.

Murphy, Brenda. "Women, Will, and Survival: The Figure in Margaret Drabble's Carpet." *South Atlantic Quarterly* 82 (1983):38–50. Traces "carnivores" and "herbivores" in the canon.

Myer, Valerie Grosvenor. "Margaret Drabble in Conversation with Valerie Grosvenor Myer." London: British Council Literature Study Aids, 1977. Recorded Interview. Highlights: Drabble wants to be readable; worries about the middle-brow reader; relates life and art; wishes God existed but afraid He does not exist; thinks that if we go on hoping and trying, will receive an answer.

Oates, Joyce Carol. "Bricks and Mortar." *Ms.*, August 1974, 34–36. Review of *Arnold Bennett* by a major novelist who proclaims one can read Drabble to know what London and England are like.

Poland, Nancy. "Margaret Drabble: 'There Must Be a Lot of People Like Me.' " *Midwest Quarterly* 16 (1975):255–67. A major interview. Drabble's looks and personality. Earlier novels on situation of being a woman, but life becomes wider with age. Serious writer who asks questions but does not preach.

Preussner, Dee. "Talking with Margaret Drabble." *Modern Fiction Studies* 25 (1979–80):563–77. Combines two worlds: classical education and everyday experience of women. Finds fate and character irreconcilable—characters must work out balance. Contrasts self with Lessing. Cannot see where fits in women's movement. Feels need to describe place. Solipsism offends.

Rayson, Ann. "Motherhood in the Novels of Margaret Drabble." *Frontiers* 3 (1978):43–46. Drabble "ushers in a new era for the woman writer in which the relationship between a mother and her children is catalytic rather than destructive."

Rose, Ellen Cronan. "Drabble's *The Middle Ground:* 'Mid-Life' Narrative Strategies." *Critique* 23 (1982):69–82. Drabble is against art imposing order on experience and seeks open narrative structures that mirror fragmentation.

———. "Margaret Drabble: Surviving the Future." *Critique* 15 (1973):5–21. Drabble and her characters accept the limitations of their humanity and accept what remains: moments of integration.

———. "Twenty Questions." *Doris Lessing Newsletter* 4 (1980):5. Kate in *The Middle Ground* is a surrogate for Lessing (and Drabble).

Rozencwajg, Iris. "Interview with Margaret Drabble." *Women's Studies* 6 (1979):335–47. Drabble on literary figures, survival, and her background, especially her husband. Considers women's liberation interesting but not something to which she would want to give much of her life or time.

Rubenstein, Roberta. "From Detritus to Discovery: Margaret Drabble's *The Middle Ground.*" *Journal of Narrative Technique* 14 (1984):1–16. An affirmative novel operating on many levels simultaneously.

Sadler, Lynn Veach. " 'The Society We Have': The Search for Meaning in Drabble's *The Middle Ground.*" *Critique* 23 (1982):83–93. Another refusal to draw conclusions. If there are answers, they seem to fall in reconciliation with the past, the family, and society generally.

Sharpe, Patricia. "On First Looking into *The Realms of Gold.*" *Michigan Quarterly Review* 16 (1977):225–31. A review of *The Realms of Gold* and Myer's *Margaret Drabble: Puritanism and Permissiveness.* Negative view of Myer.

Sherry, Ruth. "Margaret Drabble's *The Millstone:* A Feminist Approach." *Edda* 1 (1979):41–53. Drabble realistic in having Rosamund overcome some of the limits on women and then encounter other, less predictable ones.

Spitzer, Susan. "Fantasy and Femaleness in Margaret Drabble's *The Millstone.*" *Novel* 11 (1978):227–45. Genital versus maternal love. The "unruly force" of Rosamund's "unconscious desires effectively resist[s] enlightenment."

Tyler, Ralph. "*Bookviews* Talks to Edna O'Brien and Margaret Drabble." *Bookviews* 5 (1978):6–9. Drabble's desire for authenticity and her appeal to both men and women.

Updike, John. "Drabbling in the Mud." *New Yorker,* 12 January 1976, 88–90. *The Realms of Gold* "shamelessly depend upon coincidence."

Whittier, Gayle. "Mistresses and Madonnas in the Novels of Margaret Drabble." *Women and Literature* 1 (1980):197–213. Provocative discussion of the difficulties of combining maternal and erotic roles, the ease of combining motherhood and a career.

Wikborg, Eleanor. "A Comparison of Margaret Drabble's *The Millstone* with Its *Vecko-Revyn* Adaptation, 'Barnet Du Gav Mig.' " *Moderna Sprak* 65 (1971):305–11. Antidote to critics who think Drabble's work like soap operas and fiction in women's magazines.

Index

Adams, Margaret, 131
Amis, Kingsley, 15
Animal Farm, 63
Austen, Jane, 16, 46, 75, 131

Banks, Lynne Reid, 25
Beauvoir, Simone de, 9, 12
Bellow, Saul, 131
Bennett, Arnold, 1, 7, 16, 56, 61, 131, 132
Boadicea, 4
Boethius, 138n6
Brecht, Bertolt, 56
Brontë, Charlotte, 47
Brontës, 3, 134n3
Browning, Robert, 23
Bunyan, John, 8, 13, 23, 27, 29, 33, 54–63, 64, 71, 72, 77, 123, 131, 138n15
Burgess, Anthony, 130
Burney, Fanny, 23
Burton, Richard, 76
Byatt, A. S. (novelist's sister), 3

Campion, Thomas, 46, 50
Carlyle, Thomas, 29
Clare, John, 95
Coleridge, Samuel Taylor, 47, 126
Cornillon, Susan, 131
Crispin, Edmund, 131

Daniel, Samuel, 31
Dante, 49
Defoe, Daniel, 30
Dickinson, Emily, 47, 84, 129
Drabble, Adam Richard George (novelist's son), 4
Drabble, John Frederick (novelist's father), 2
Drabble, Joseph (novelist's son), 4
Drabble, Margaret, age of heroines, 7, 134n7; and the accidental, 18, 105; and alchemy, 135n2; and art, 136n10; and chance, 1, 2, 39; and children, 3–4, 12, 23, 26, 44, 45, 53, 60–61, 77, 117; and community, 23, 59, 61, 71, 72, 75, 79, 96, 99, 124–29; and continua, 12, 33, 43, 44, 52, 76, 79, 84, 96; and diffi-

culty, 2, 10, 23, 24, 69; and endurance, 3, 65, 68, 72; and the experimental novel, 5; and fate, 1, 2, 3, 18, 39, 43, 44, 50, 51, 78, 90; and grace, 2, 3, 44, 55, 68; and literature, 3, 6, 29–32, 46–49, 121–24, 129; and luck, 1, 2, 3, 5, 7, 10, 18, 27, 38, 39, 44, 51, 54, 57, 62, 68, 80, 91, 93, 124; and marriage, 5, 7, 11–12, 13, 61, 64, 73–88; and men, 7, 10, 11, 20–21, 67–70, 98–99, 125–27; and mothers, 2, 12, 17, 40, 51, 65, 111–12, 125; and the *Oxford Companion to English Literature,* 6, 130, 138n14; and paradox and ambiguity, 1, 15, 16, 22, 26, 45; and the past, 2, 8, 41, 89, 92, 121–24; and privilege vs. inequality, 1, 2, 6, 7, 10, 15, 16, 32, 34, 38, 51, 63–65, 66, 68, 70, 83; and public causes/universal concerns, 6, 7, 8, 53, 70, 101, 104, 127; and the Quakers, 2, 14, 136n5; and rigidity, 18–19, 27–29, 76; and solipsism, 2, 6, 23, 33, 46, 80; and stereotyping, 11, 48, 49, 51, 69, 86–87, 99; and "strain tells," 17, 21, 33, 65; and the "unlovely," 2, 7–8, 93, 115; and willing events to occur, 17, 19, 29, 86, 96, 108; and women's liberation and issues, 1, 4, 6, 7, 11, 12, 21, 26, 27, 32, 36, 37, 38, 39, 48, 49, 53, 63, 66–67, 69, 76–79, 84, 86, 90, 91, 92, 94, 99–100, 111, 115–16, 125–27, 131–32, 137n1, 138n3, n8; animal imagery, 11, 31, 34, 39–40, 53, 54, 56, 58–59, 75, 78, 79, 82, 83, 91, 92, 94, 96, 97–98, 99, 103, 104, 105–6, 107, 109, 111, 115, 117, 119, 120; aureate imagery, 14, 18, 19, 23, 33, 40, 43, 57, 68, 69, 90, 97; background of, 1; bird imagery, 3, 11, 13, 14, 22, 43, 56, 71, 76, 86, 103, 109, 110, 112, 114, 115, 119; childhood of, 4; children of, 4; the Drabble person, 23, 38, 41–44, 47, 51, 57, 63, 68, 69, 70, 72, 74, 77, 83, 85, 90, 99, 108, 117; education of, 2, 4; entrapment/imprisonment imagery, 10–12, 13, 14, 22, 29, 34, 43, 53, 104, 111–12, 114, 115,

150

.